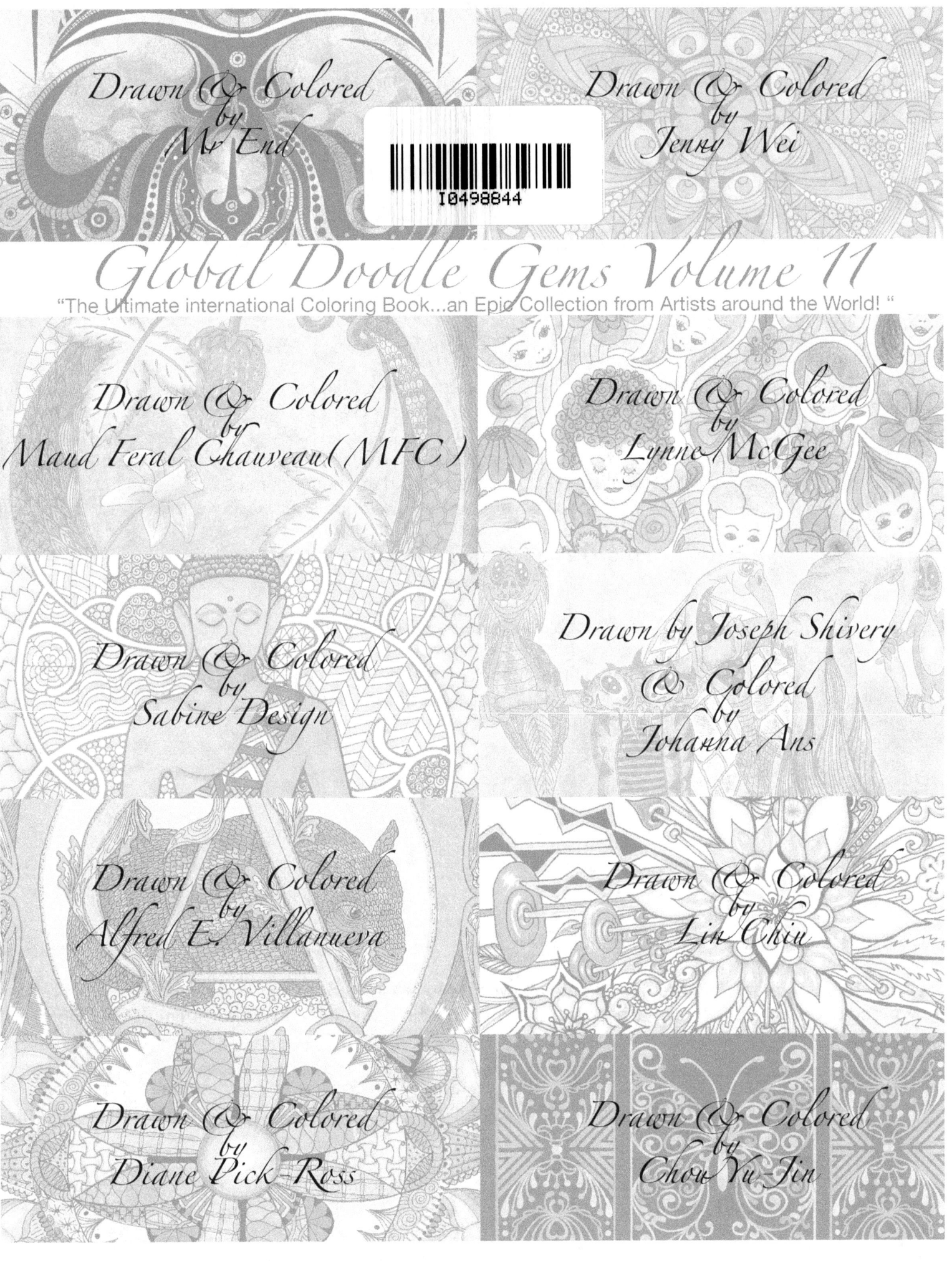

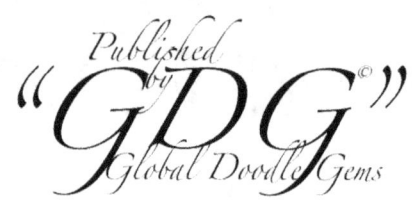

Share your colored versions with us ! We love seeing your results and hearing from you we are social !

The Official FB book page, stay on top of what we have in the works !
www.facebook.com/globaldoodlegems

The Community group, share your colored pages, meet the artists, enjoy exclusive freebies, take part in community Charity books and so much more......
www.facebook.com/groups/globaldoodlegems/

Follow us on Twitter.... @GlobalDoodlegem

We are on Instagram too
@globaldoodlegems for instagram

...and if you are not social like that we have a blog
globaldoodlegems.wordpress.com

Copyright © 2016 Global Doodle Gems

All rights are reserved by Global Doodle Gems.

Duplication of pages for personal use are allowed. You are invited to color the pages then scan/post your coloured versions to social networks, mentioning the book title and author/artist (Global Doodle Gems).

All artwork and images are protected by copyright laws. This book or any portion thereof may not, otherwise, be reproduced and/or distributed or transmitted without the express written permission of the artist/publisher of Global Doodle Gems.

All of us from the Global Doodle Gems wish you a colortastic time and look forward to seeing your wonderful color results online !

Chapter 1
Maud Feral Chauveau (MFC)

Chapter 2
Joseph Shivery

Chapter 3
Lynne McGee

Chapter 4
Alfred E. Villanueva

Chapter 5
Lin Chiu

Chapter 6
Jenny Wei

Chapter 7
Mr End

Chapter 8
Sabine Design

Chapter 9
Diane Pick-Ross

Chapter 10
Chou Yu-Jin

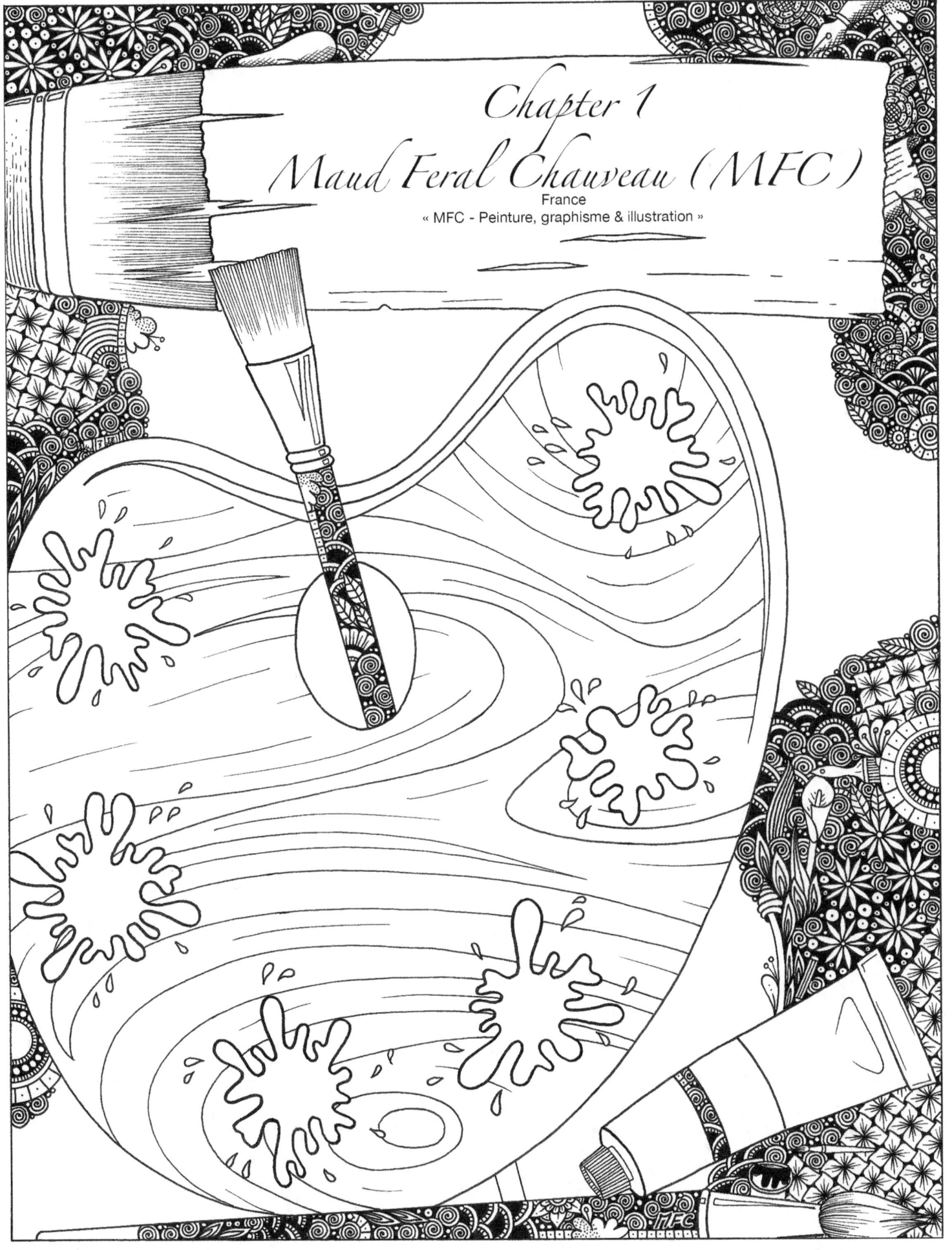

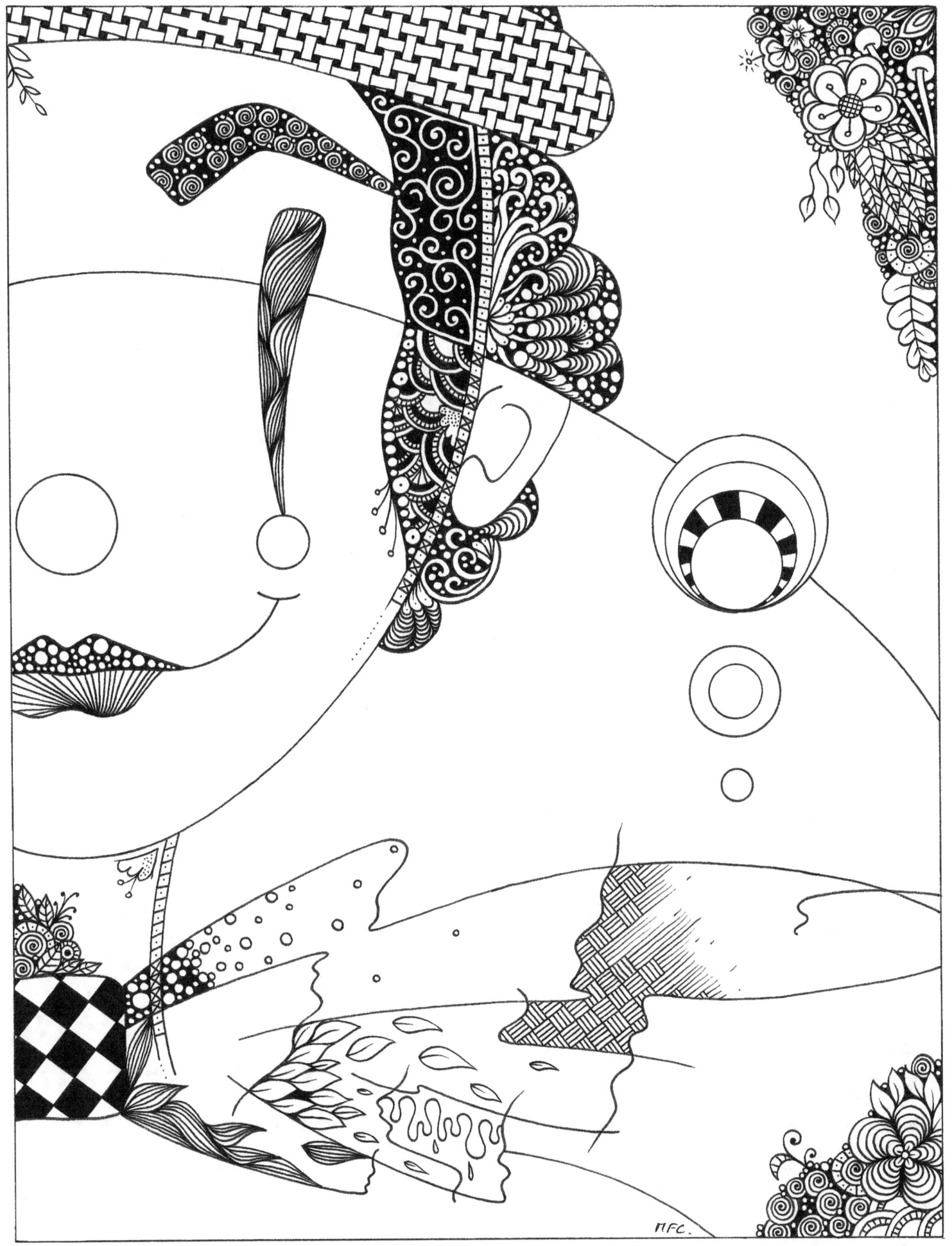

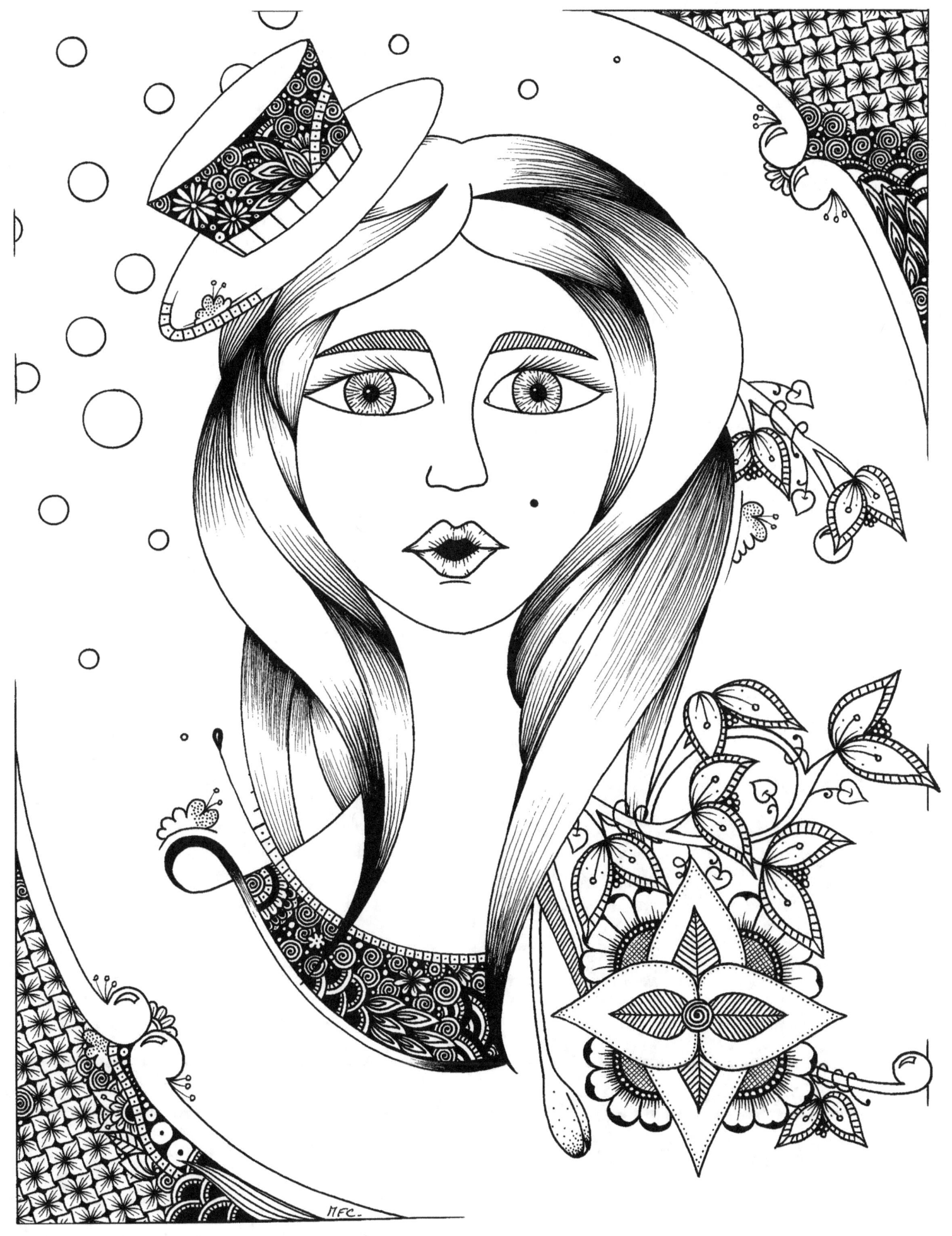

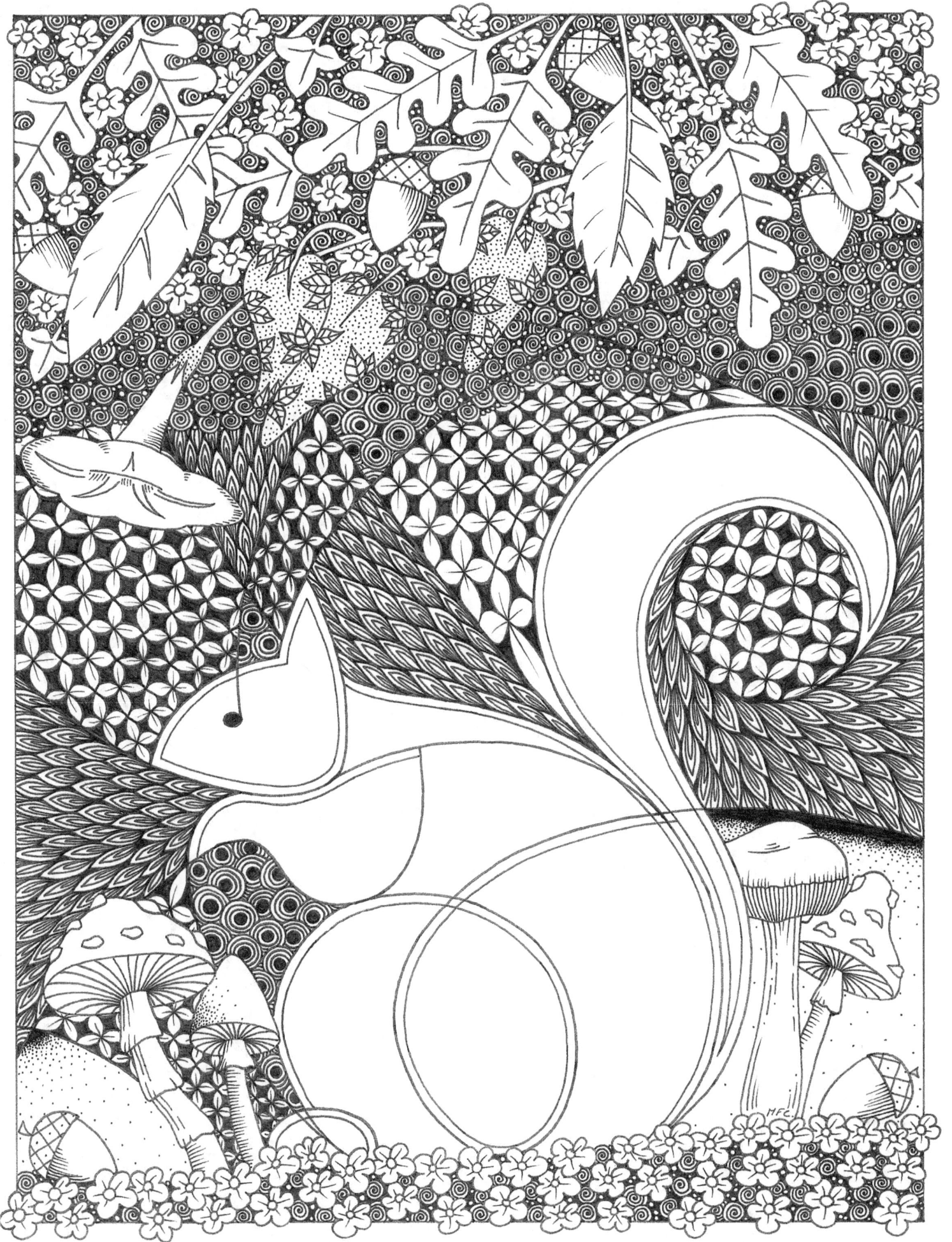

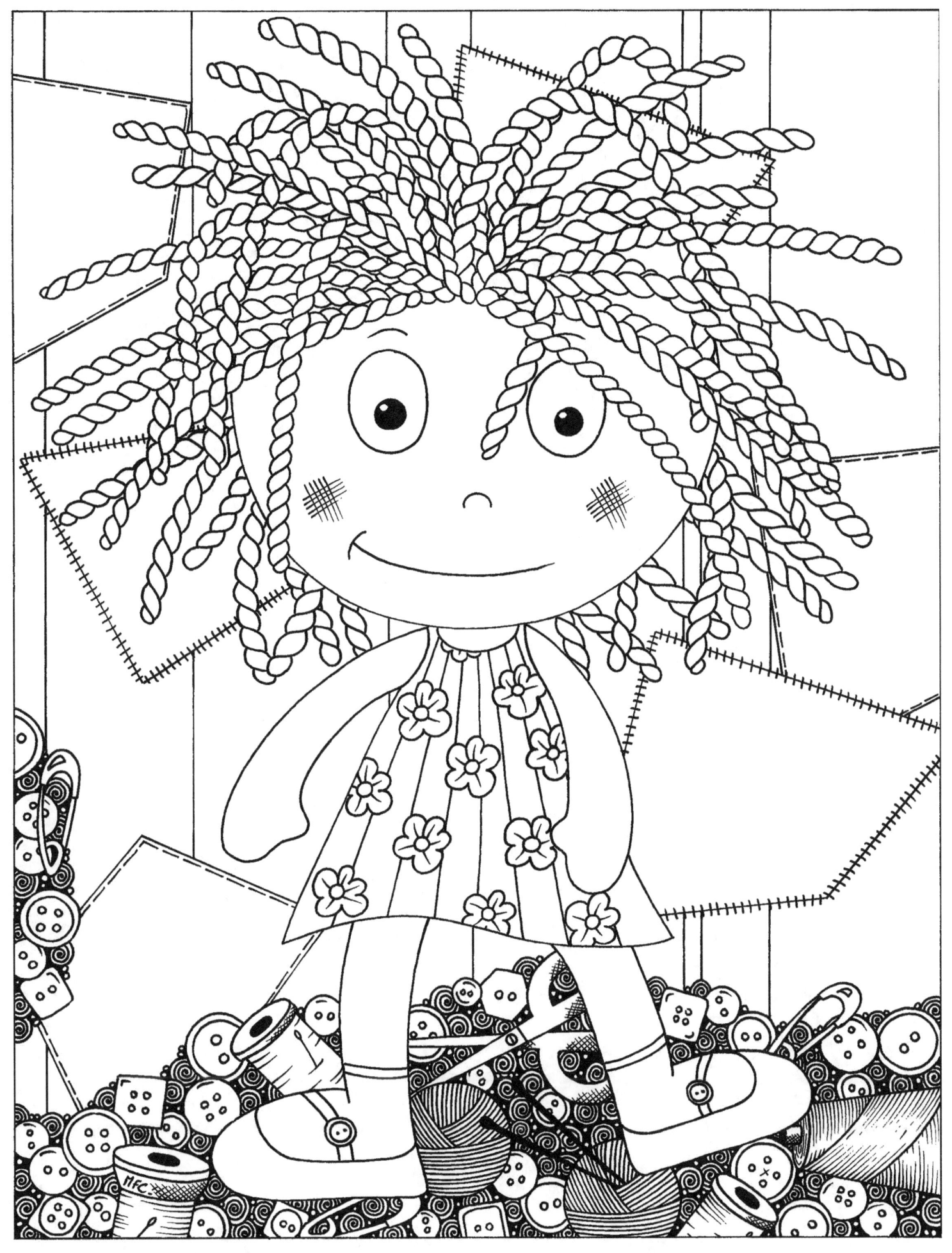

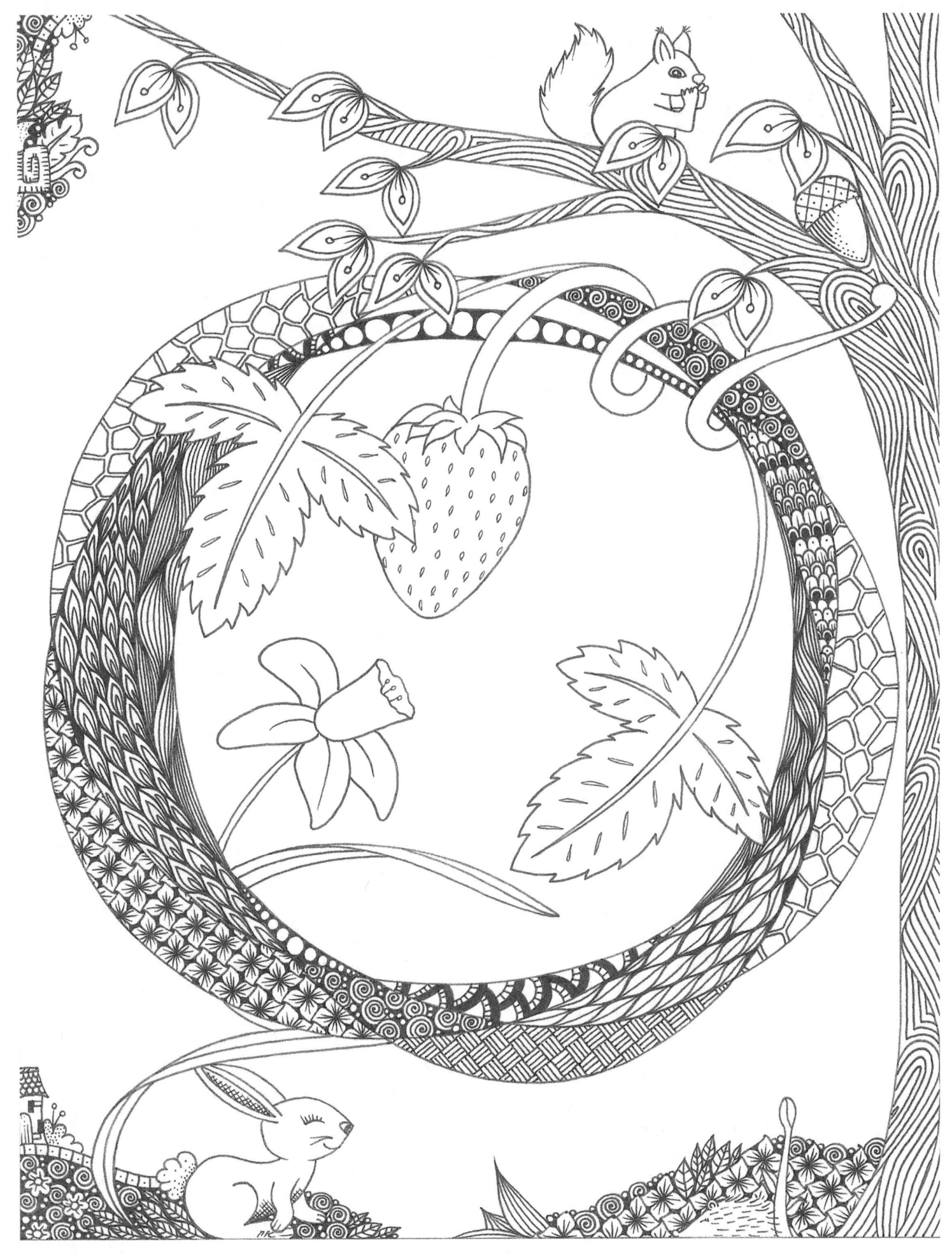

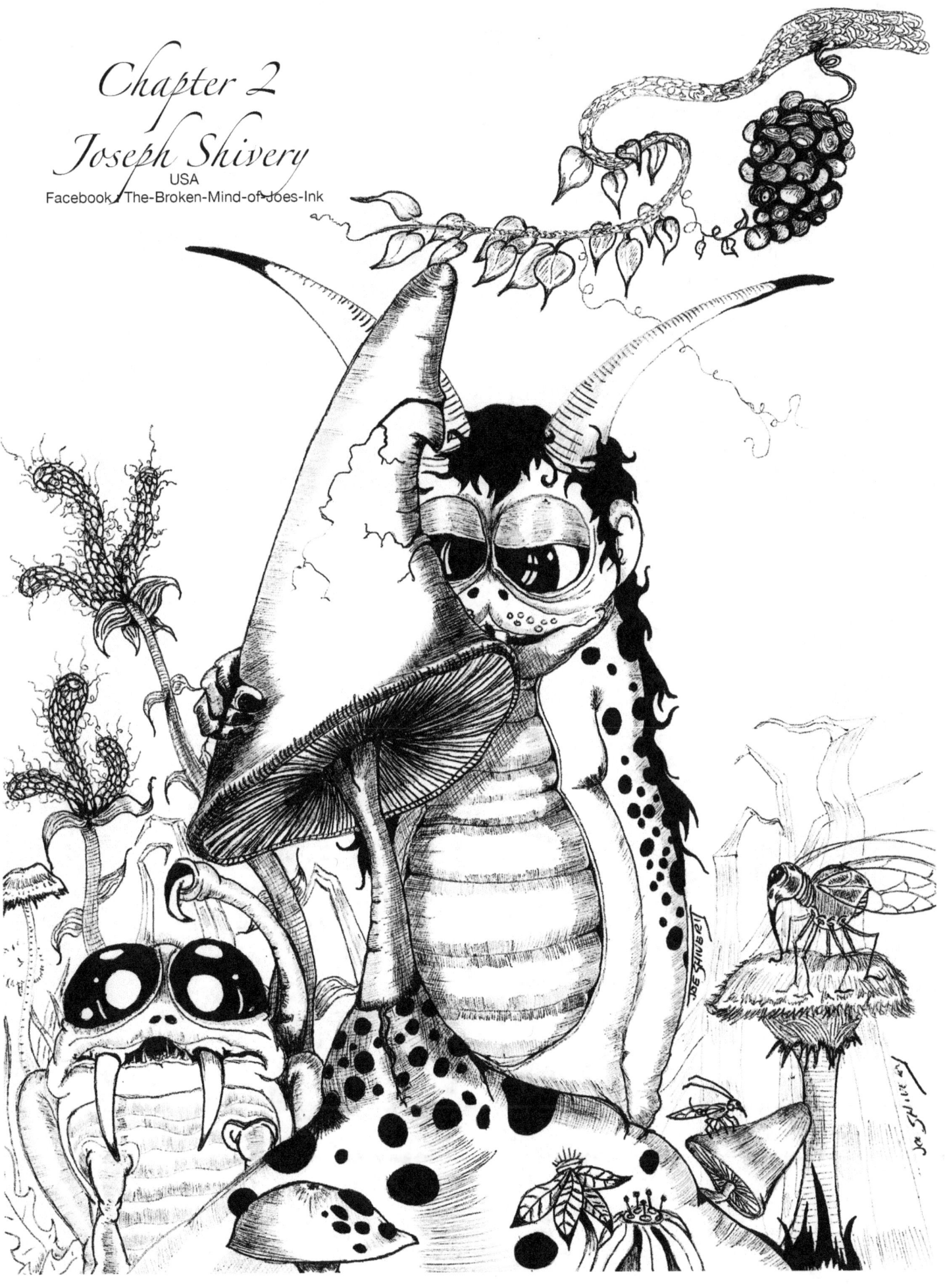

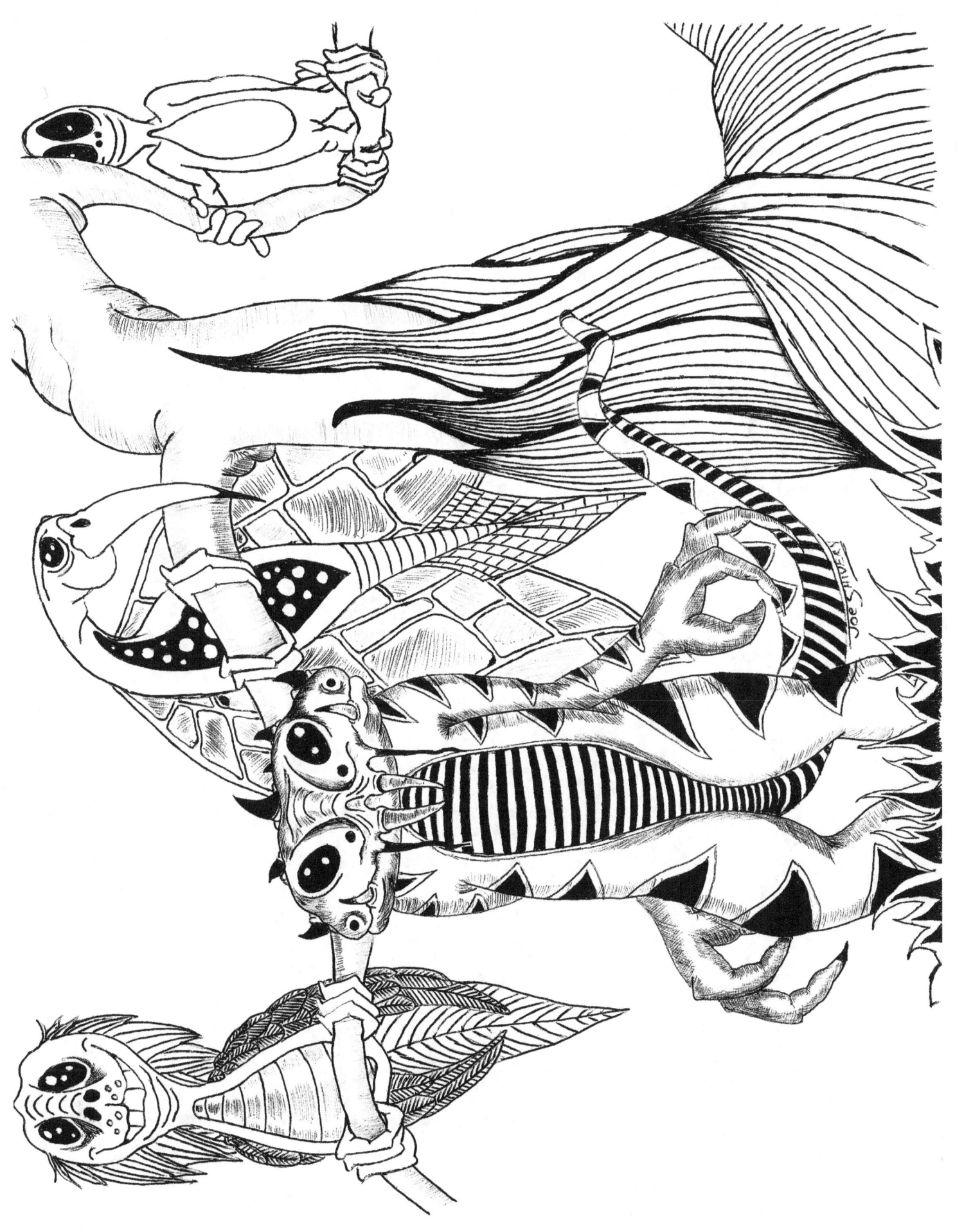

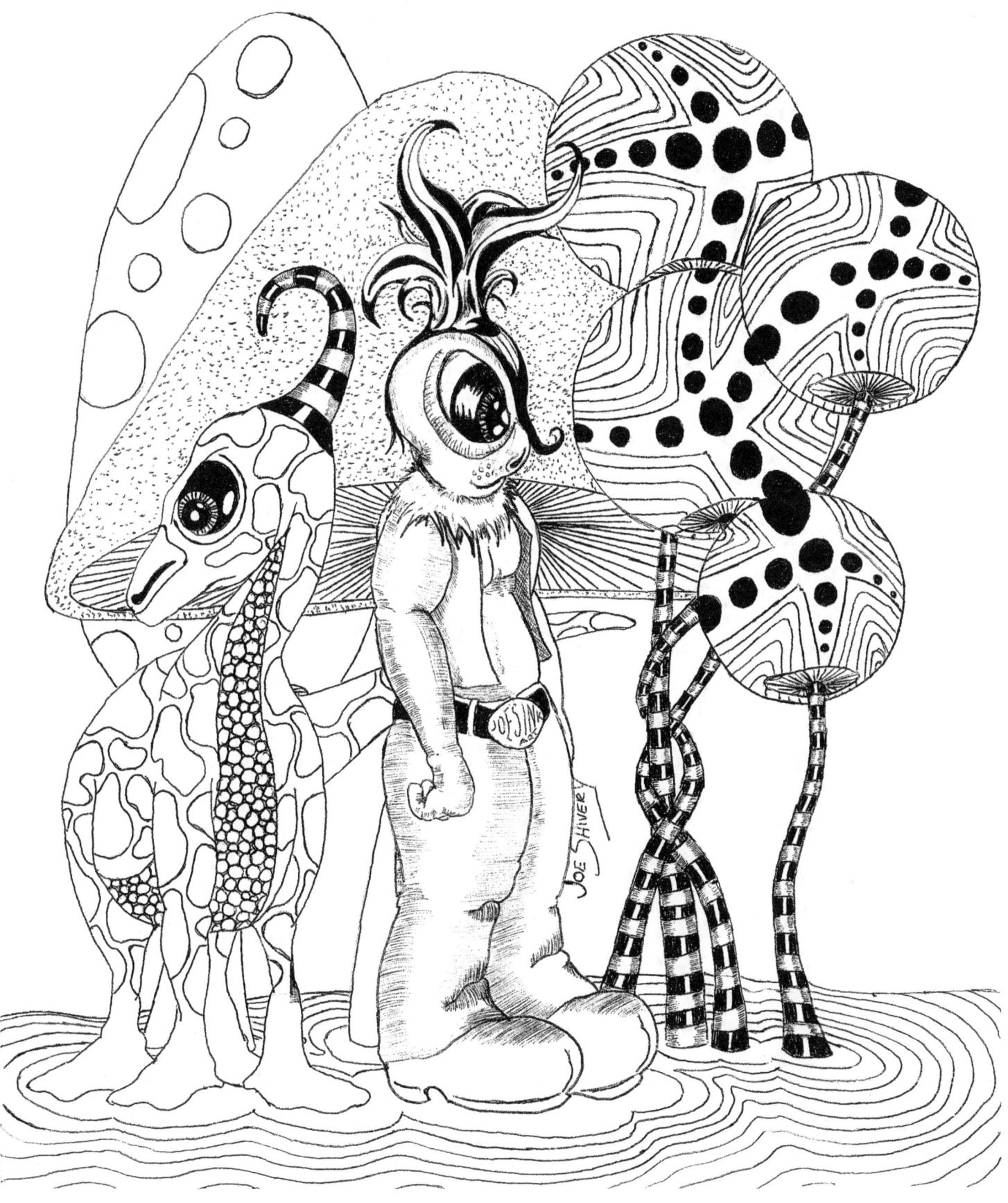

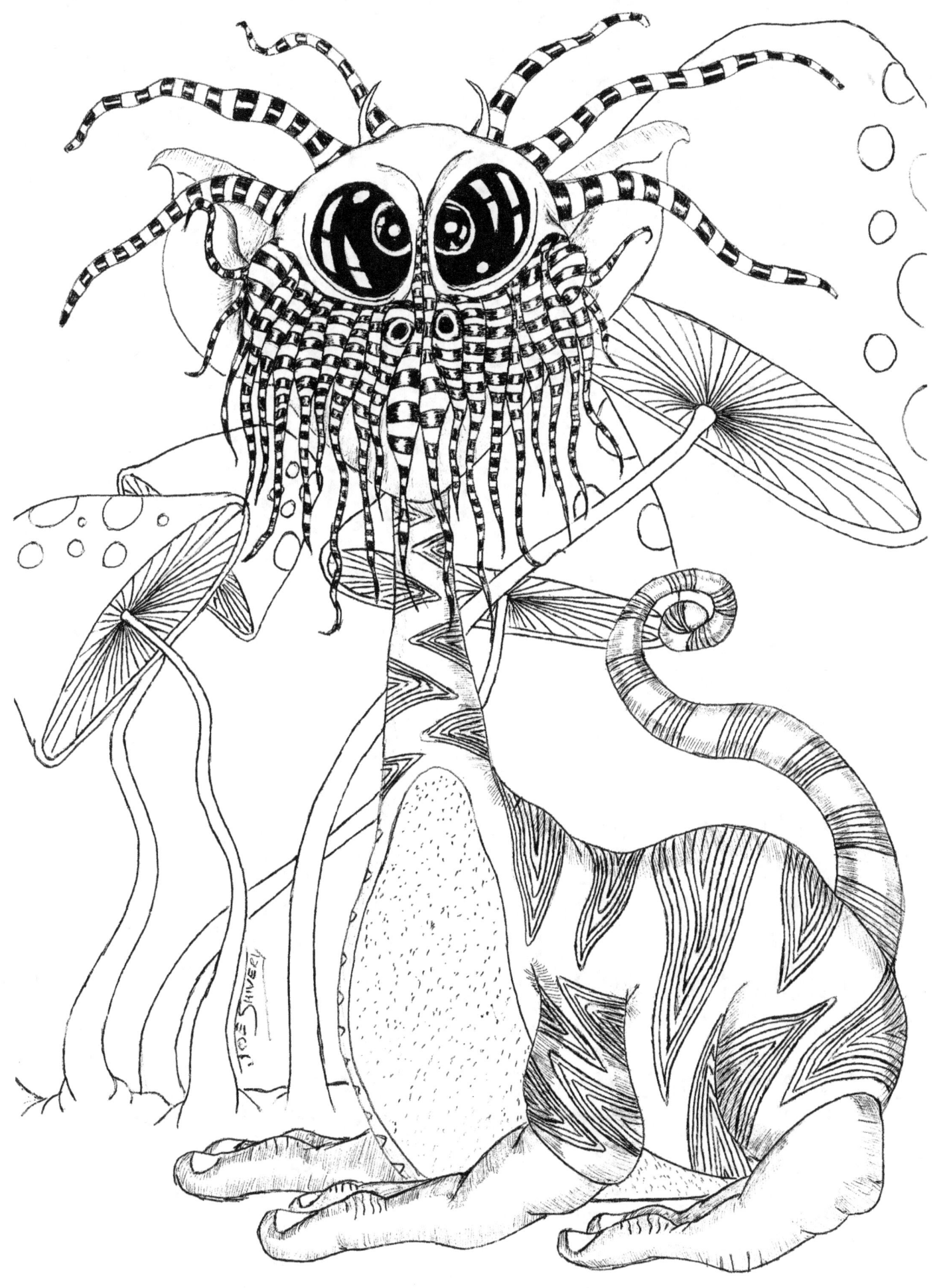

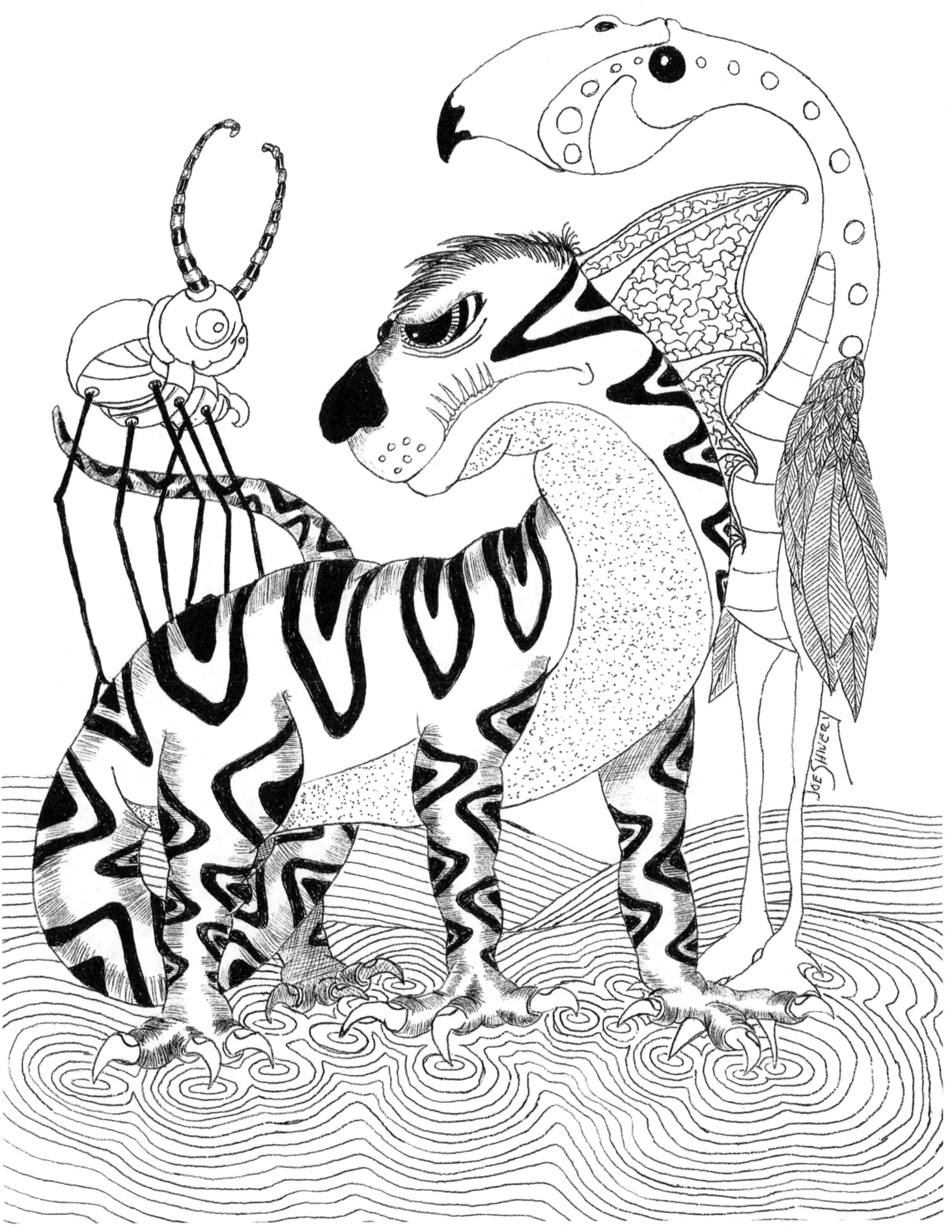

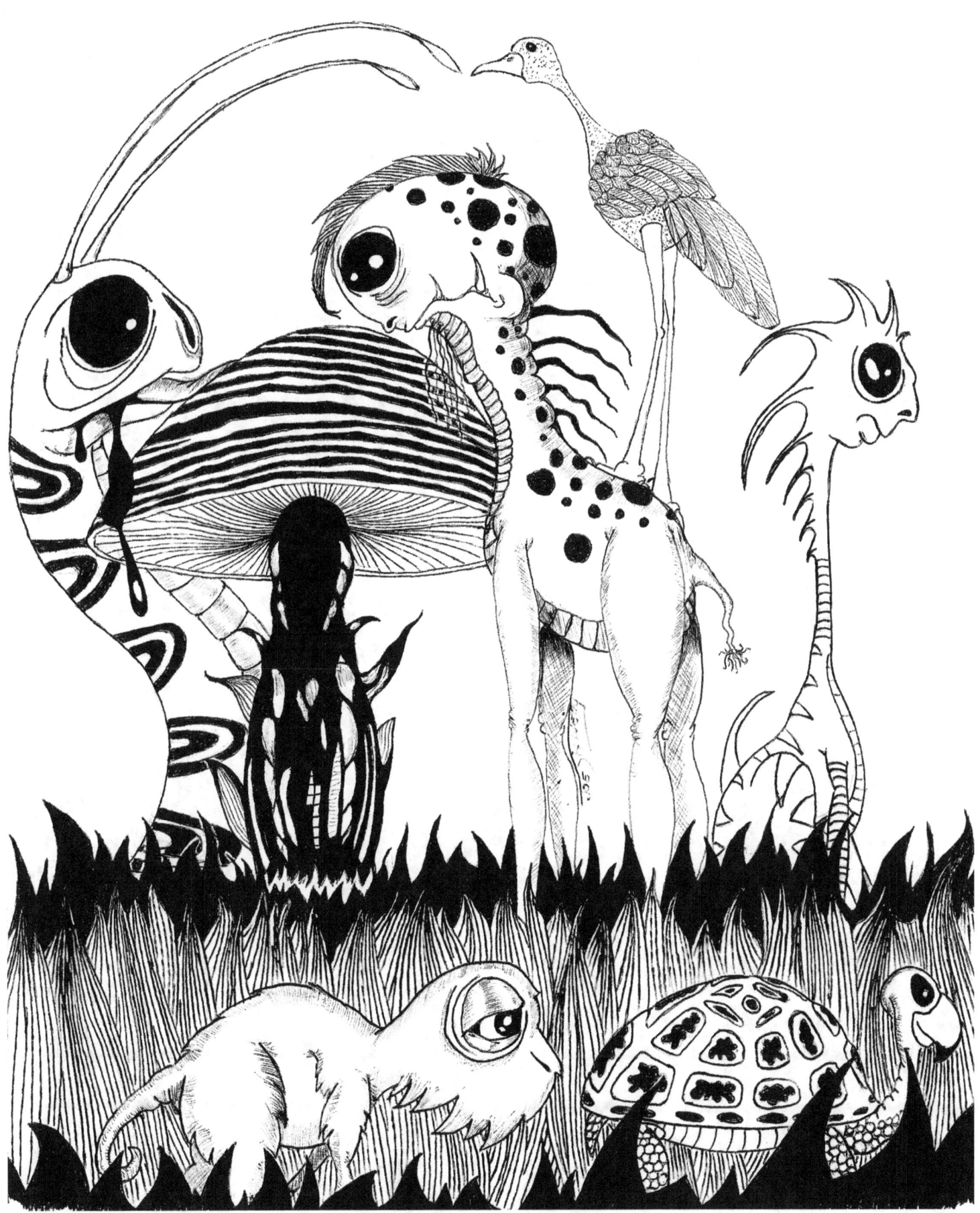

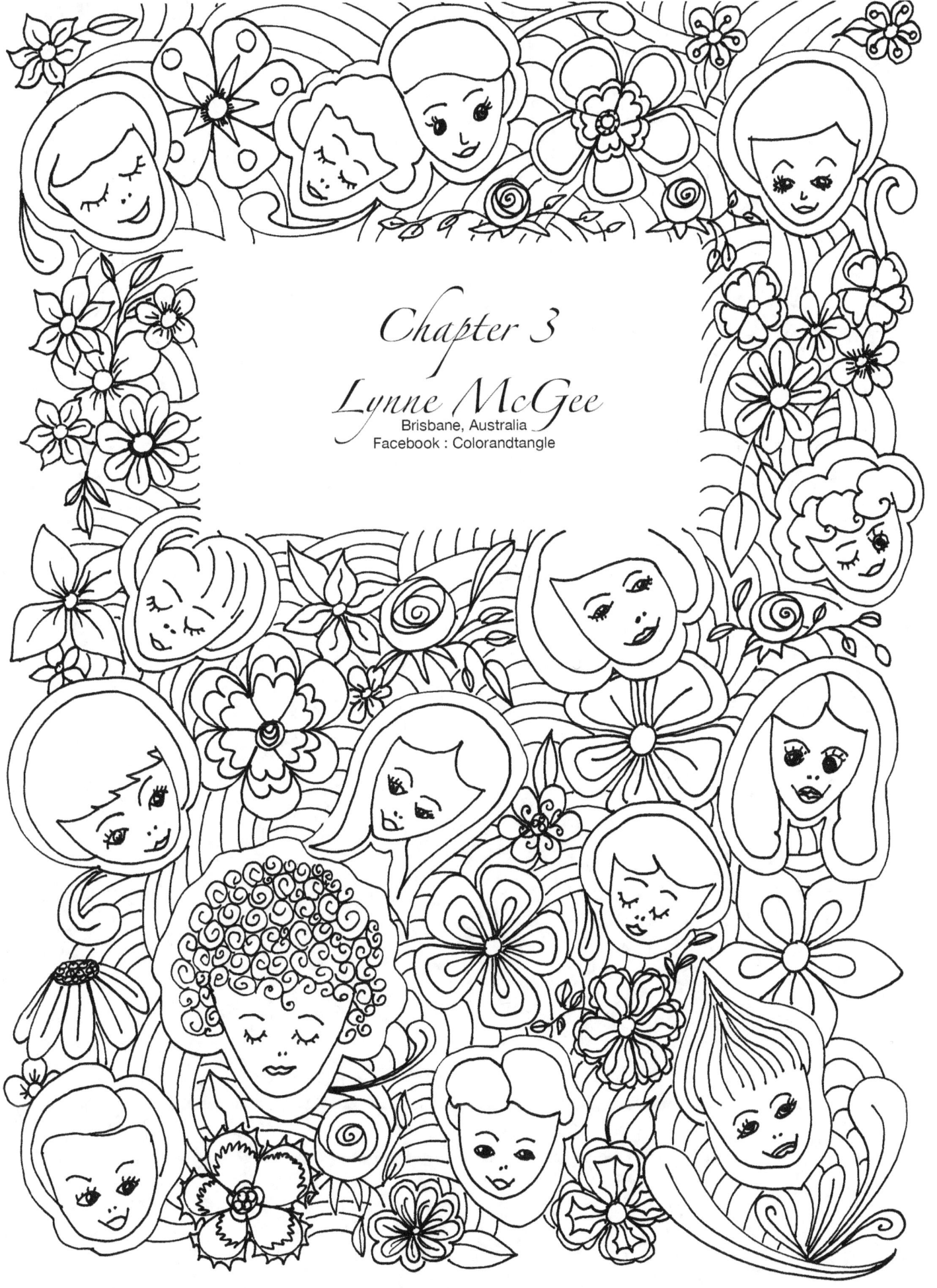

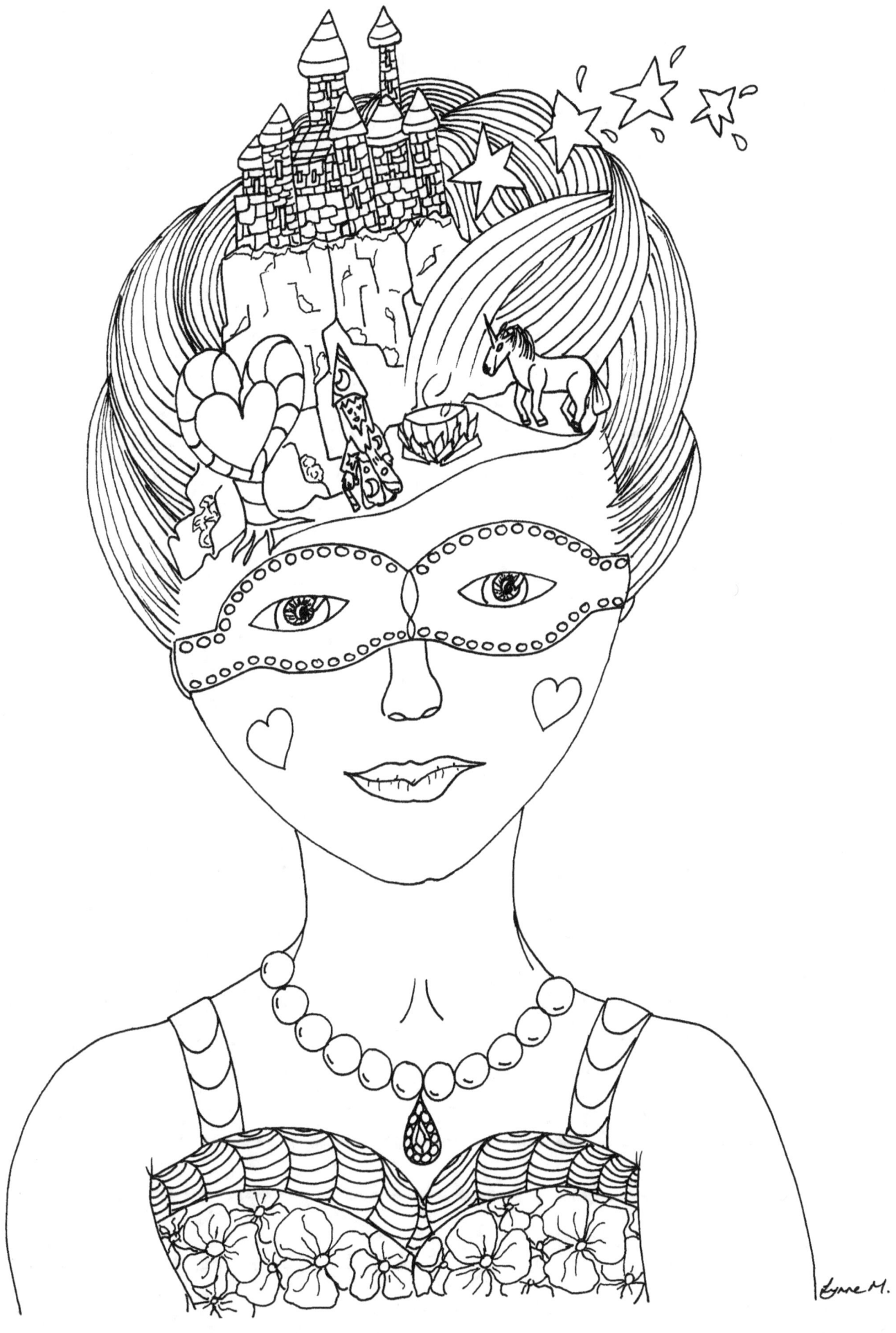

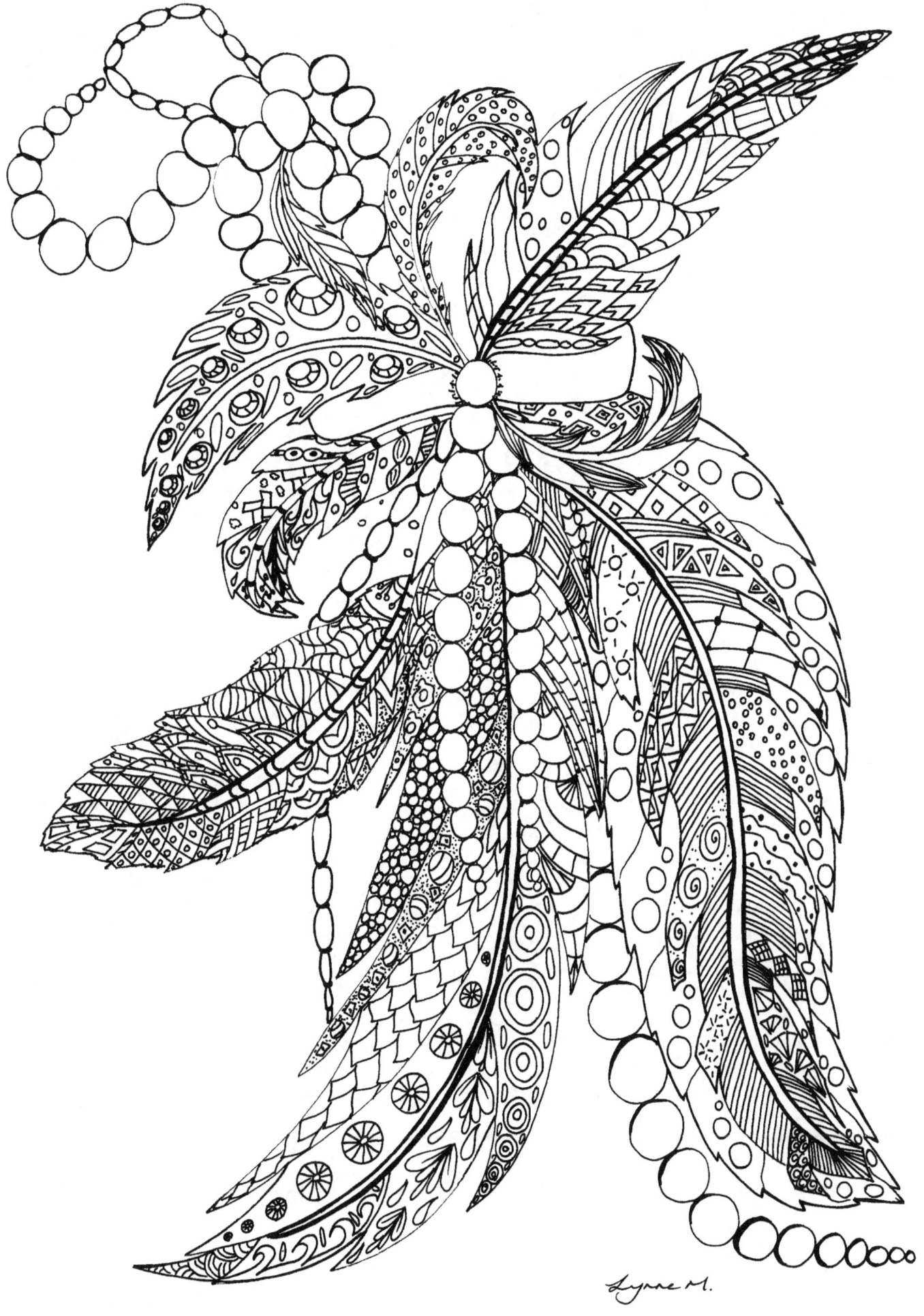

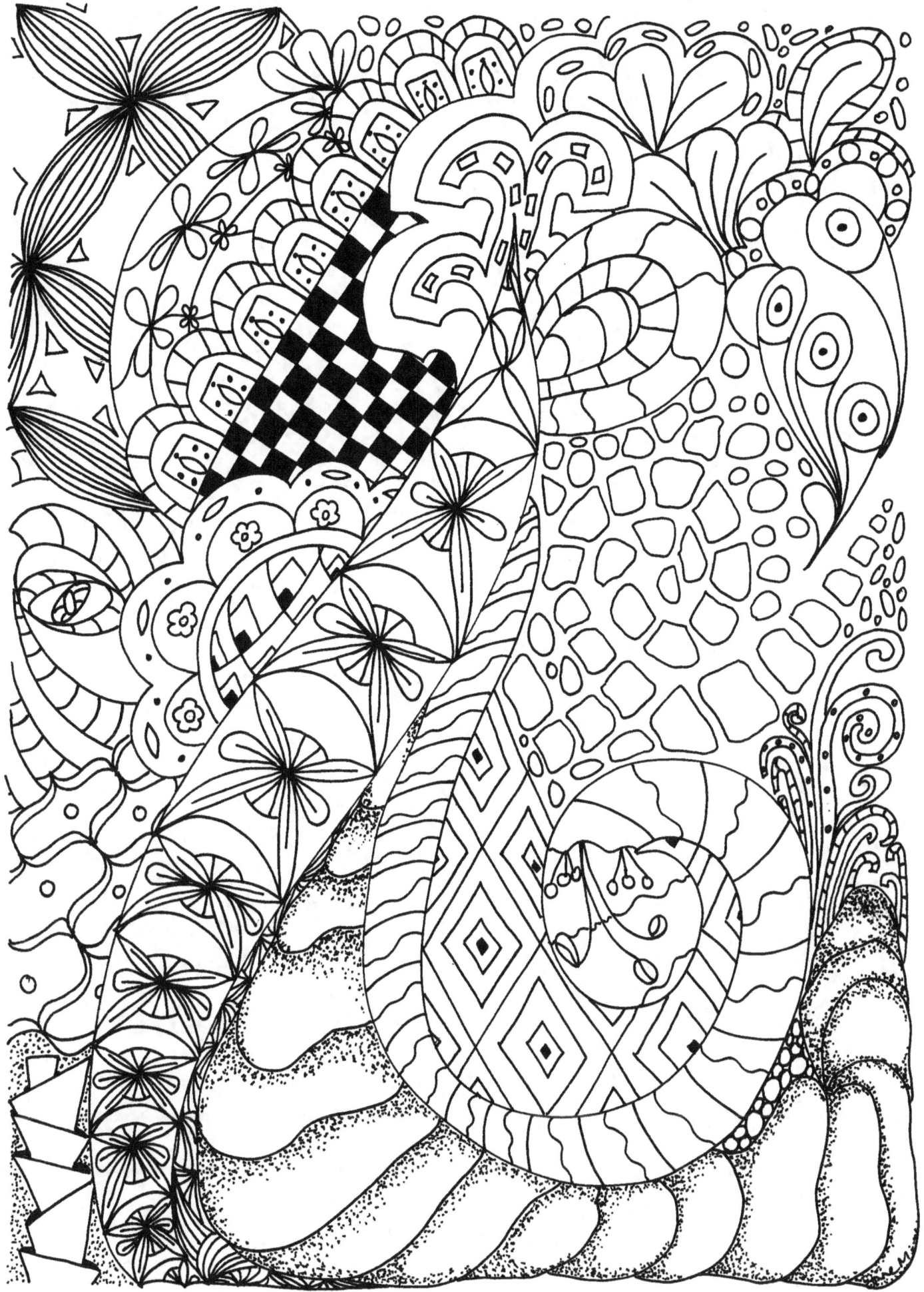

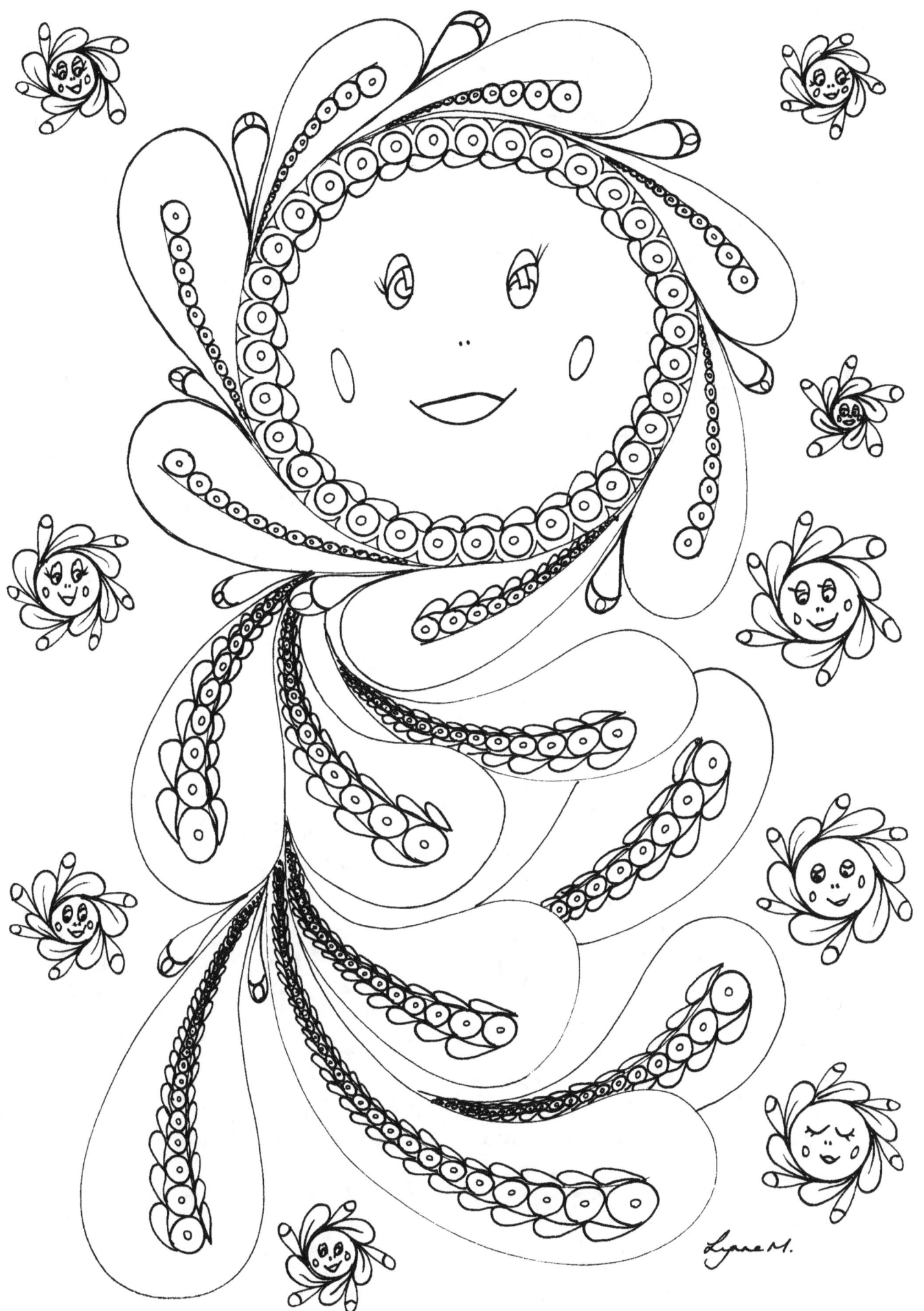

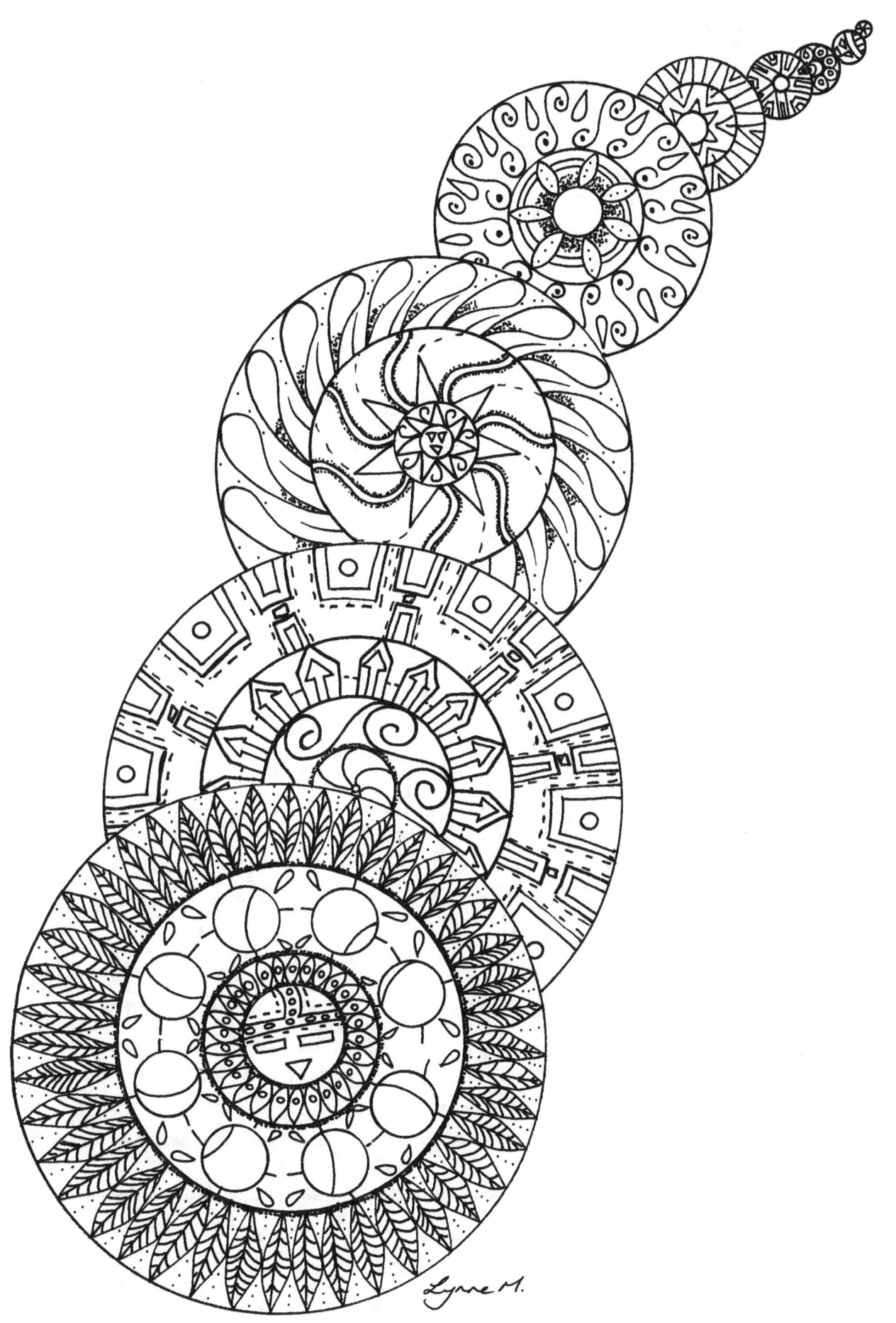

Chapter 4
Alfred E. Villanueva
Philippines
Facebook : viworksart

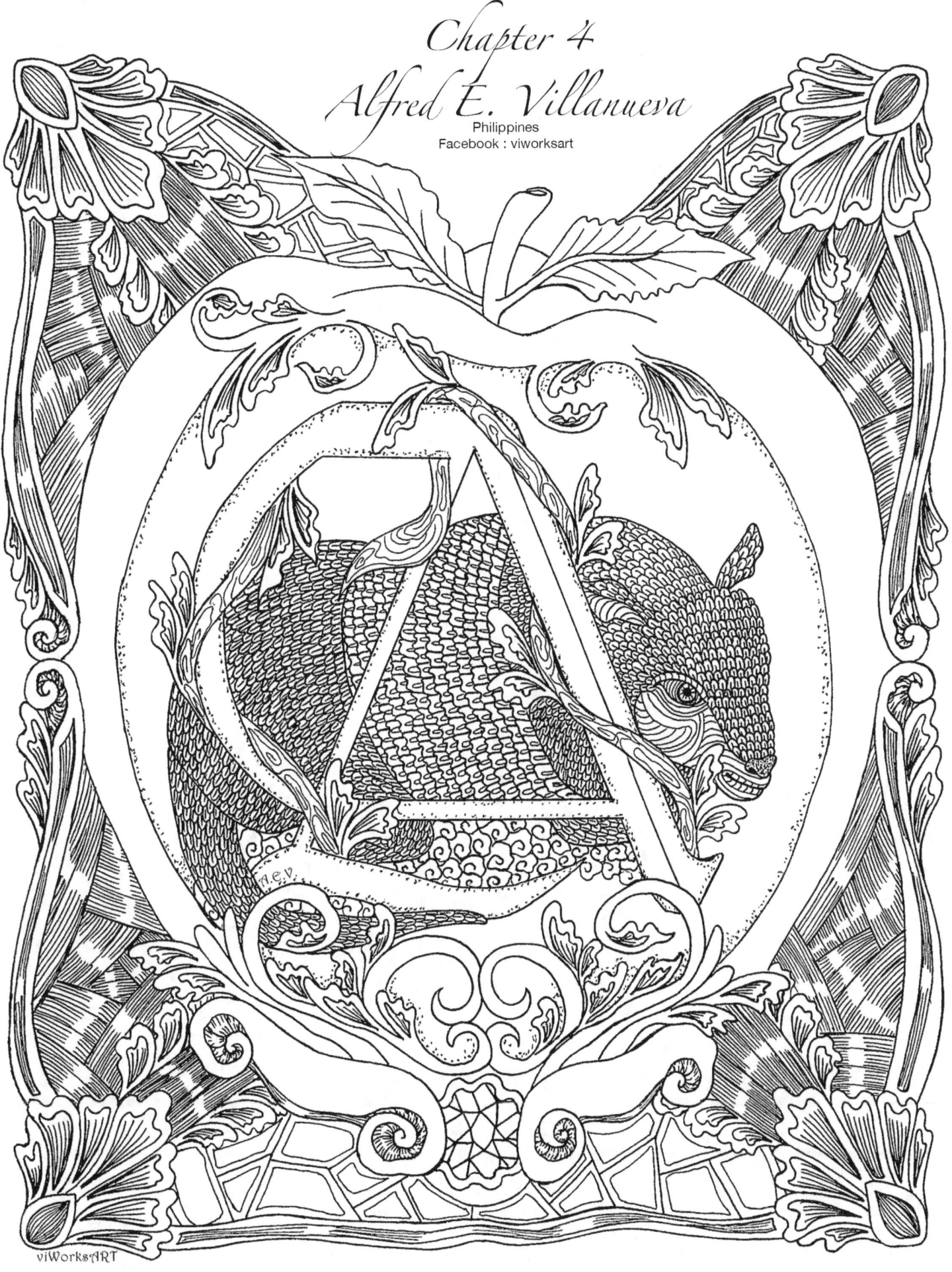

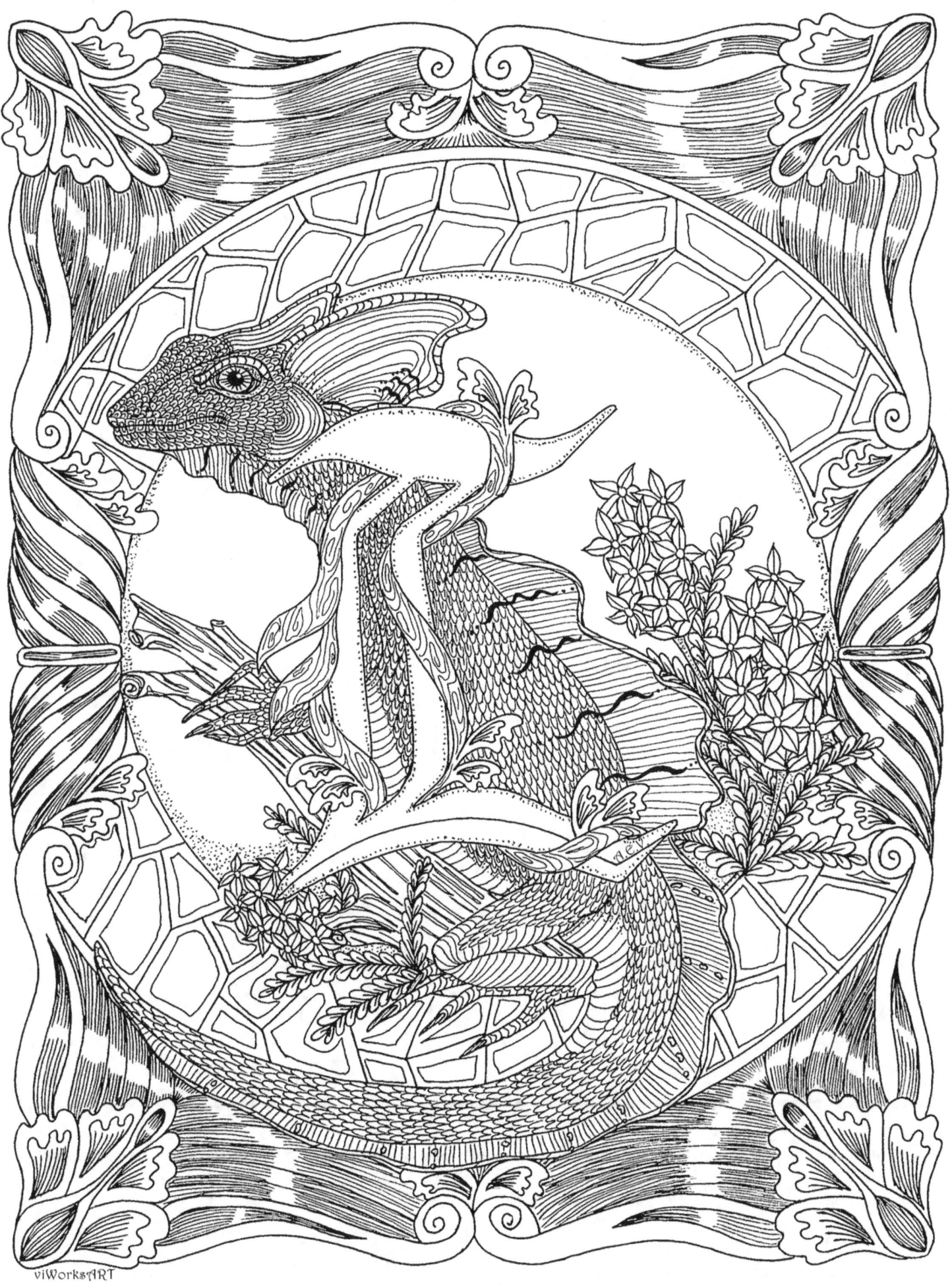

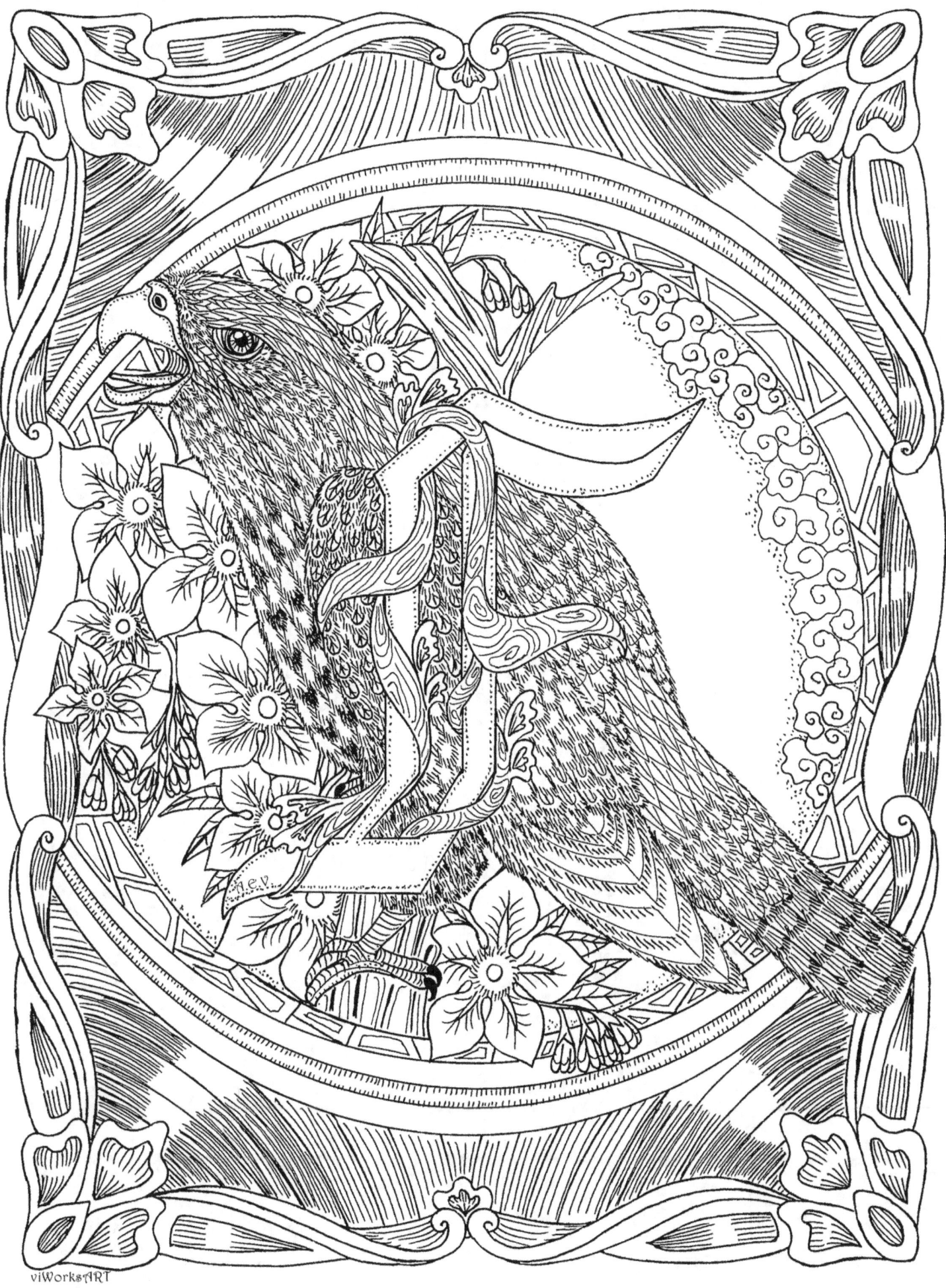

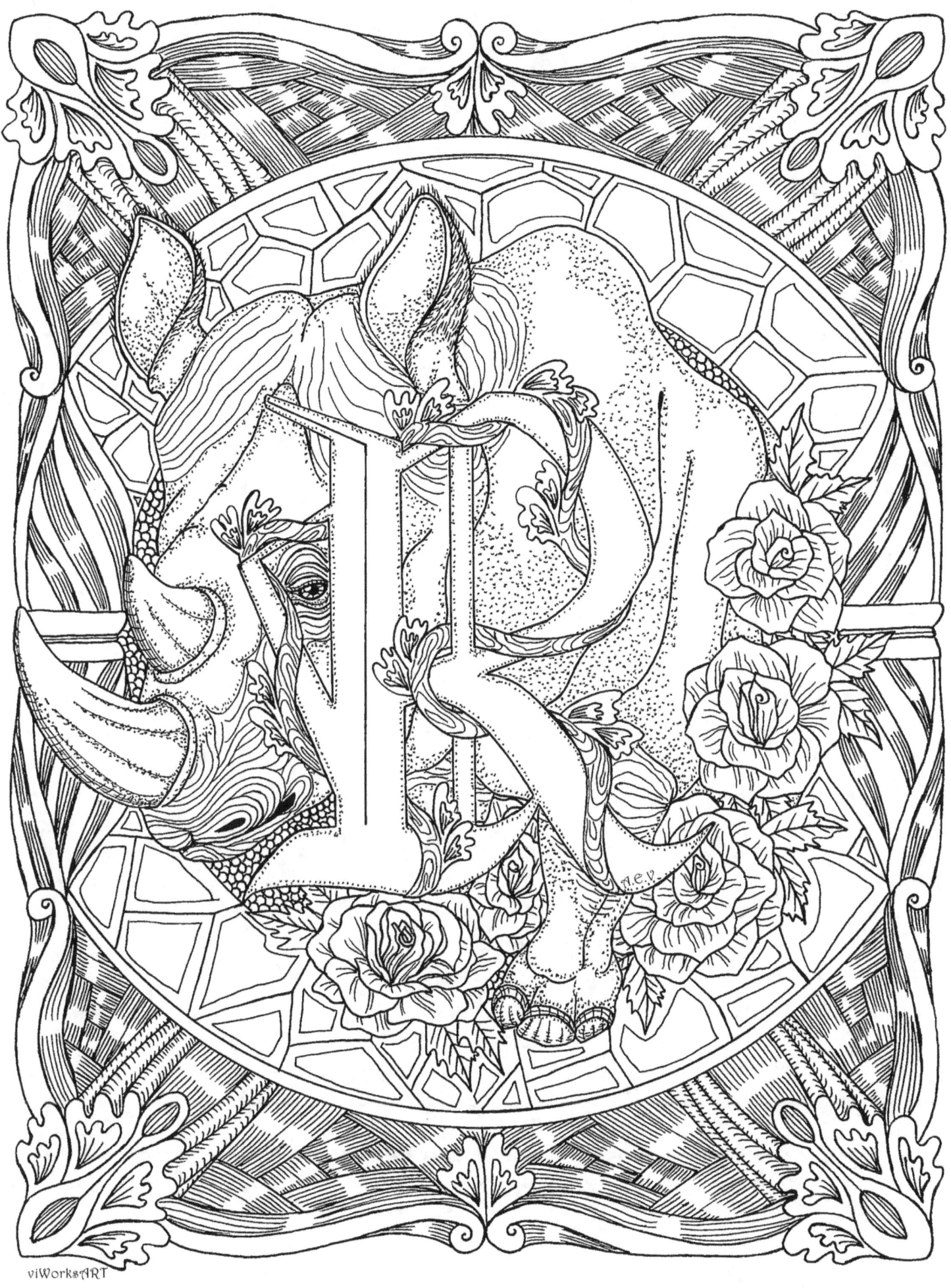

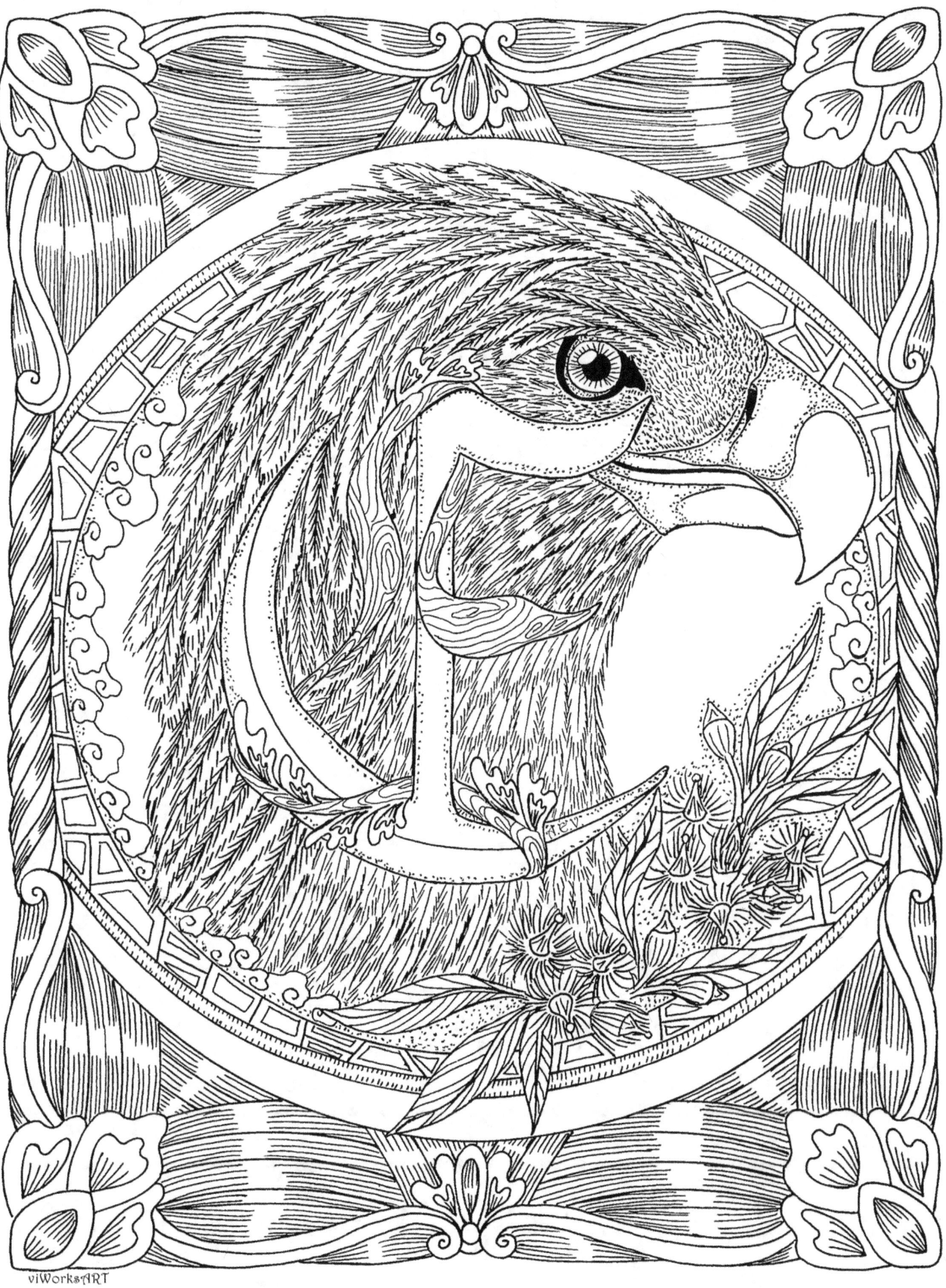

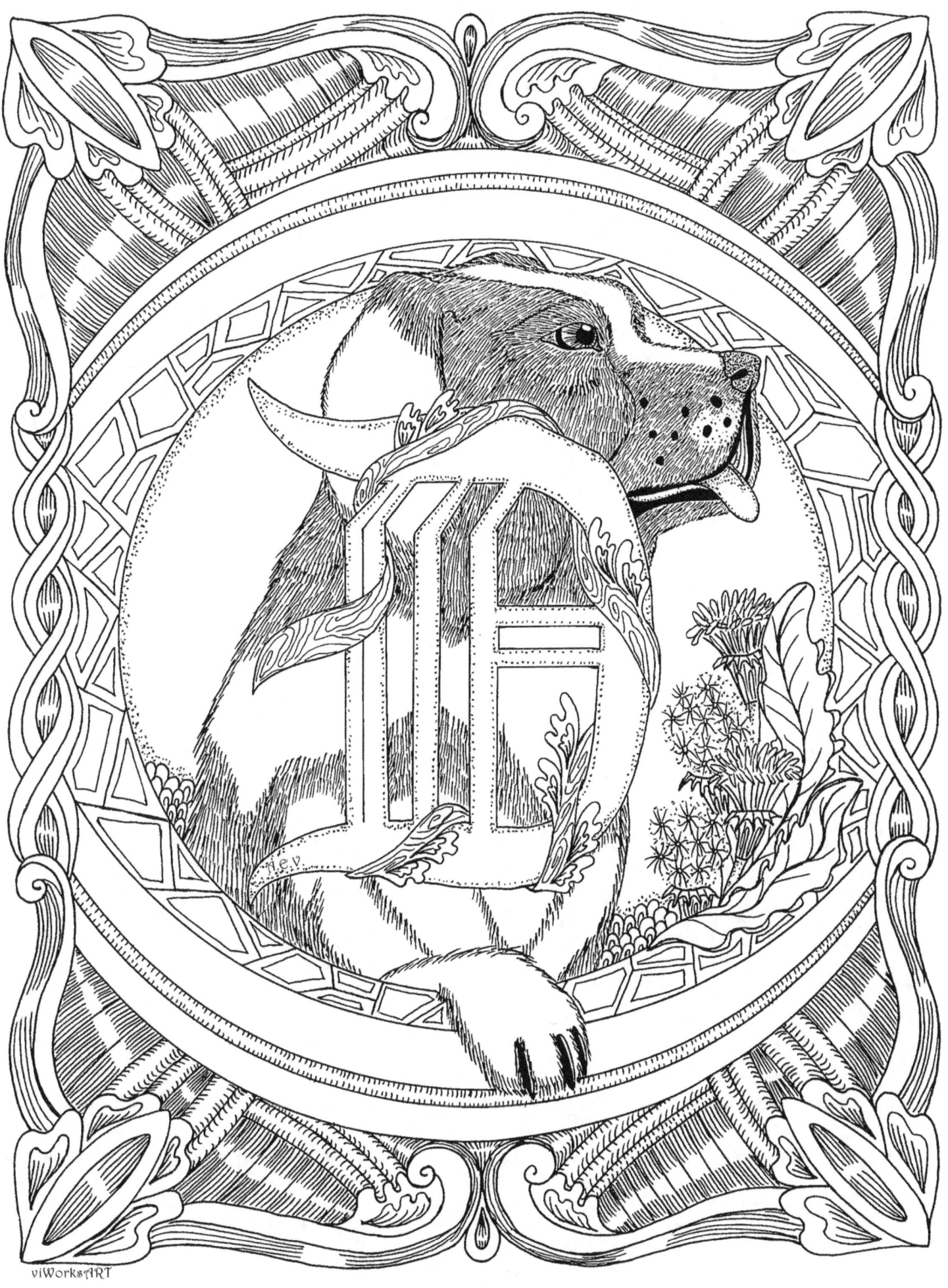

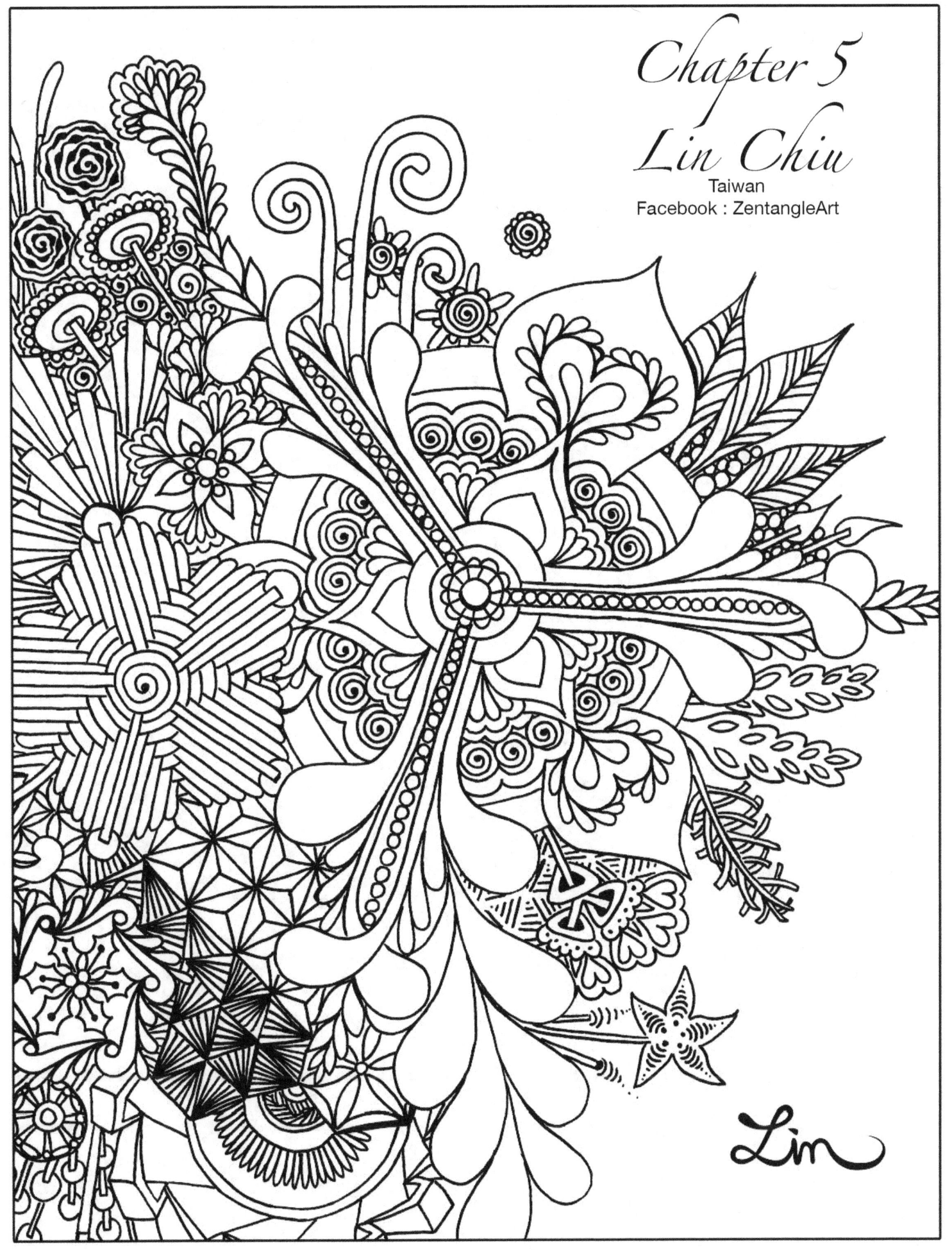

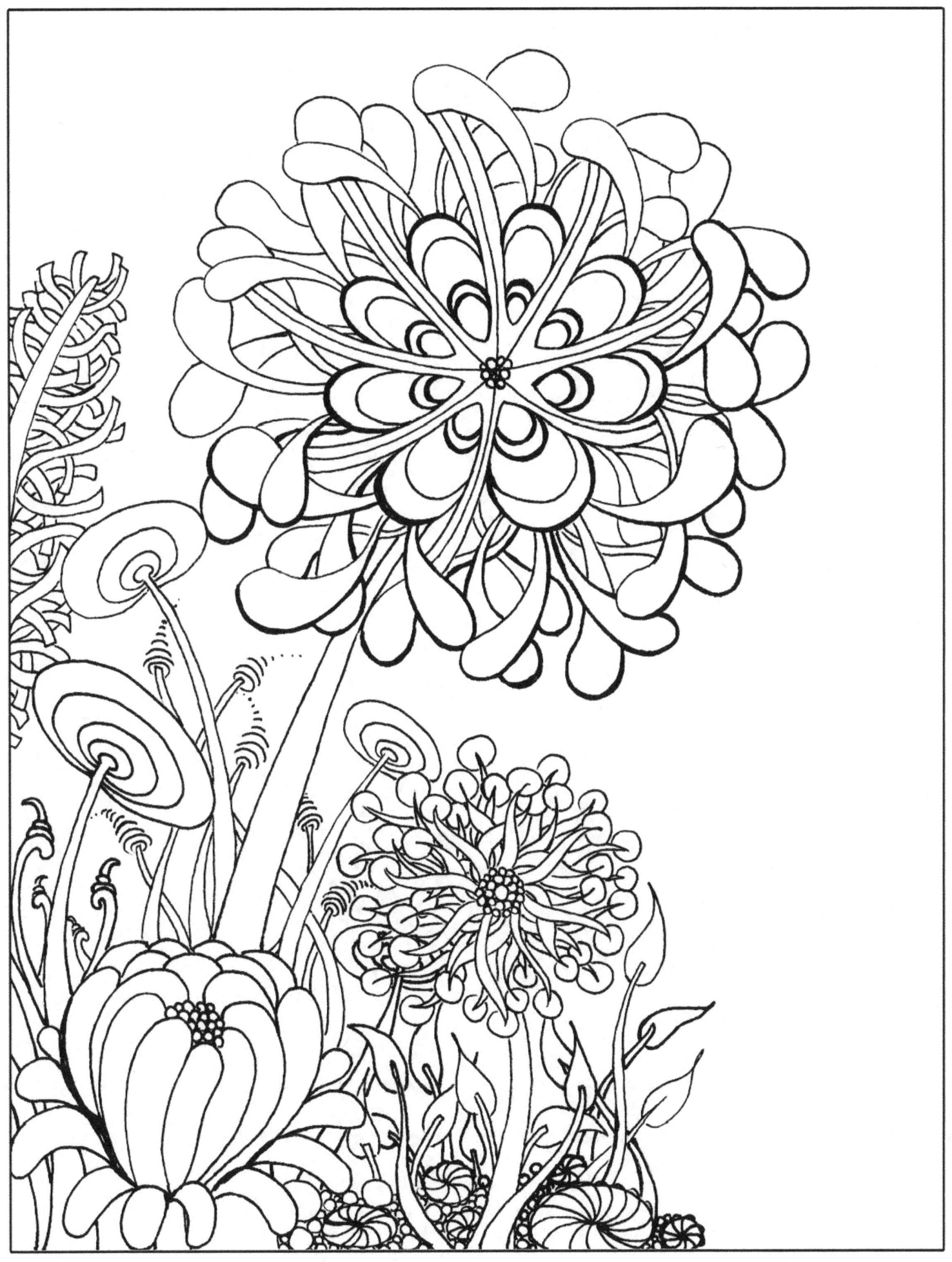

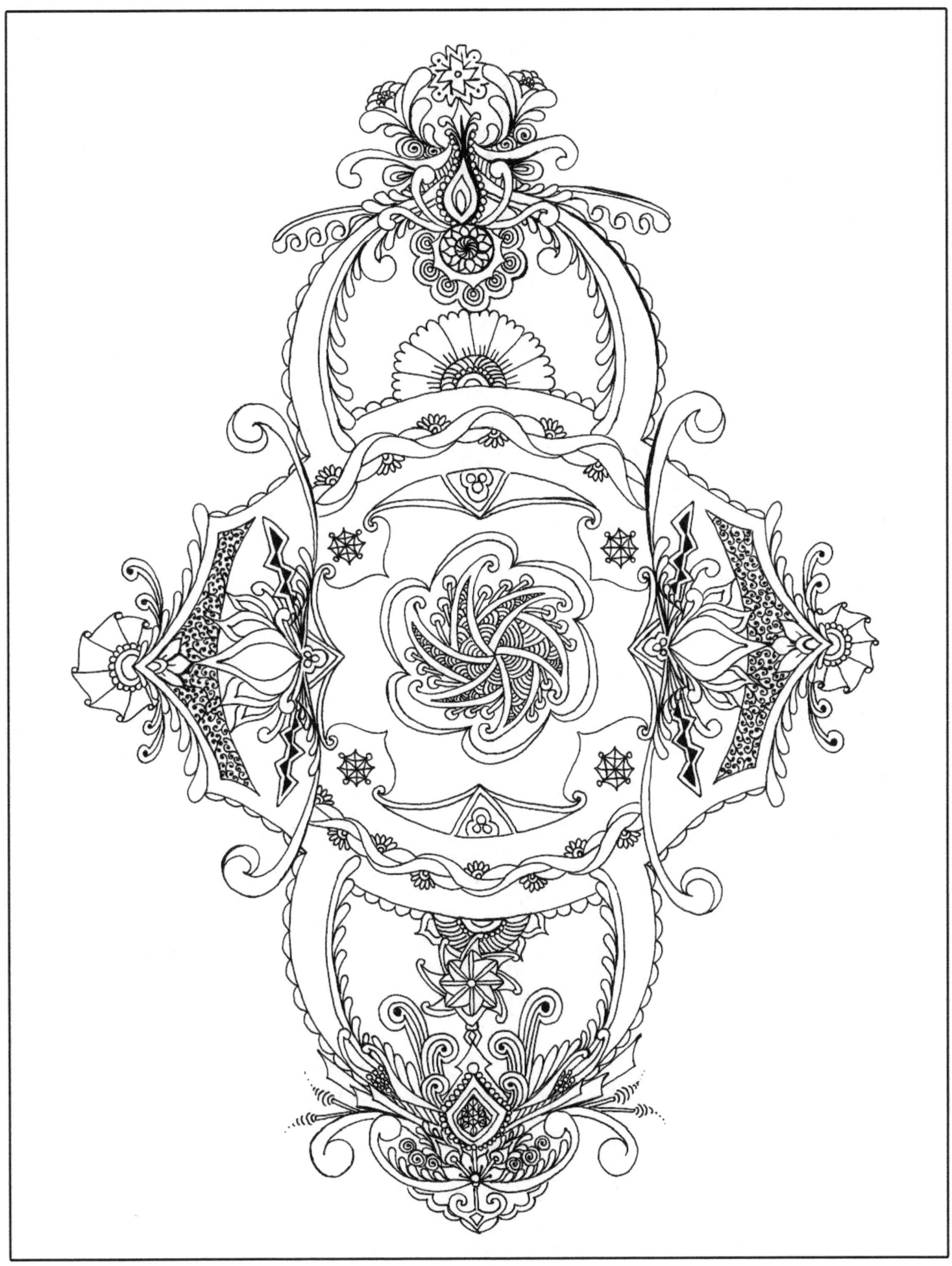

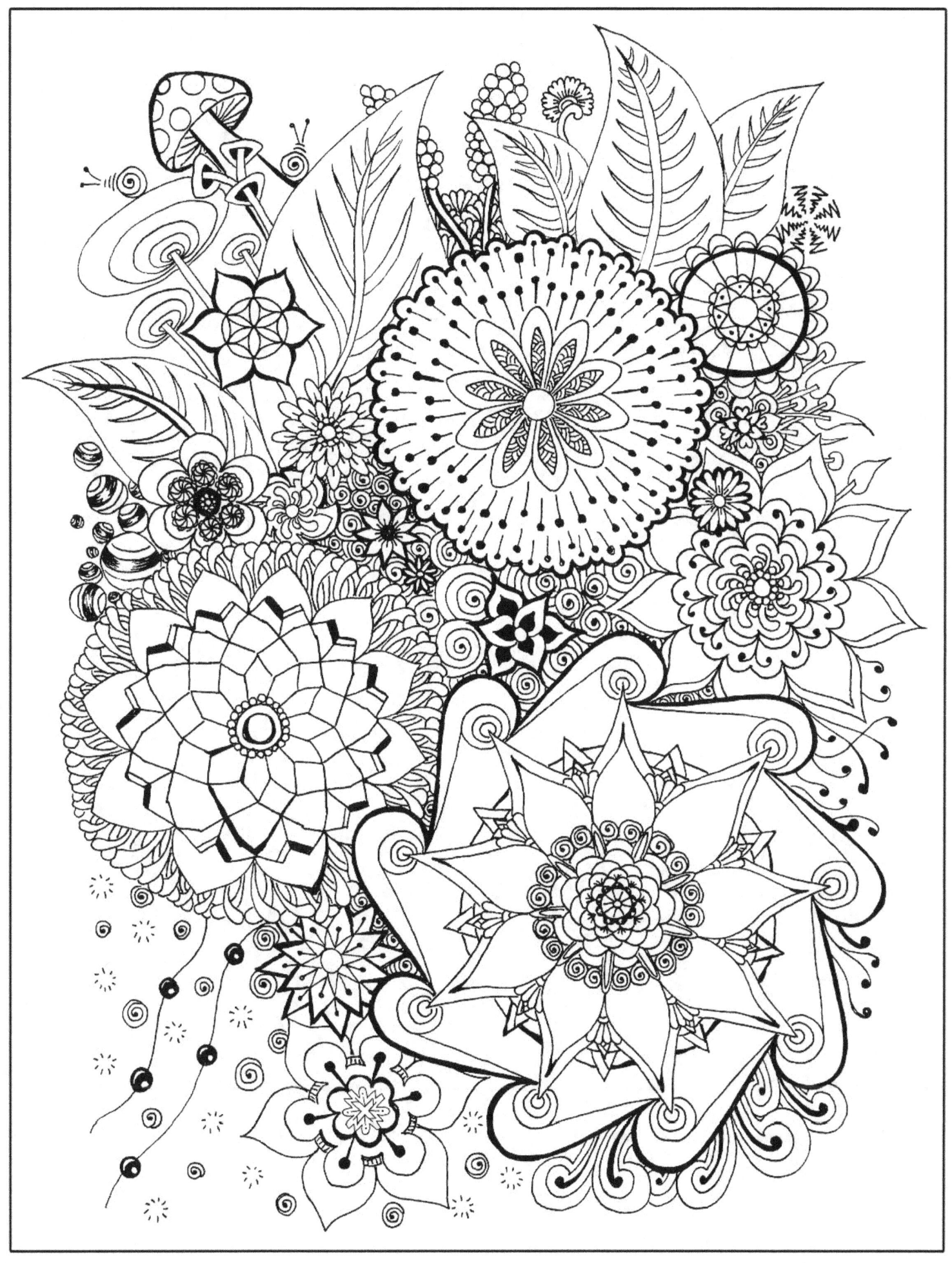

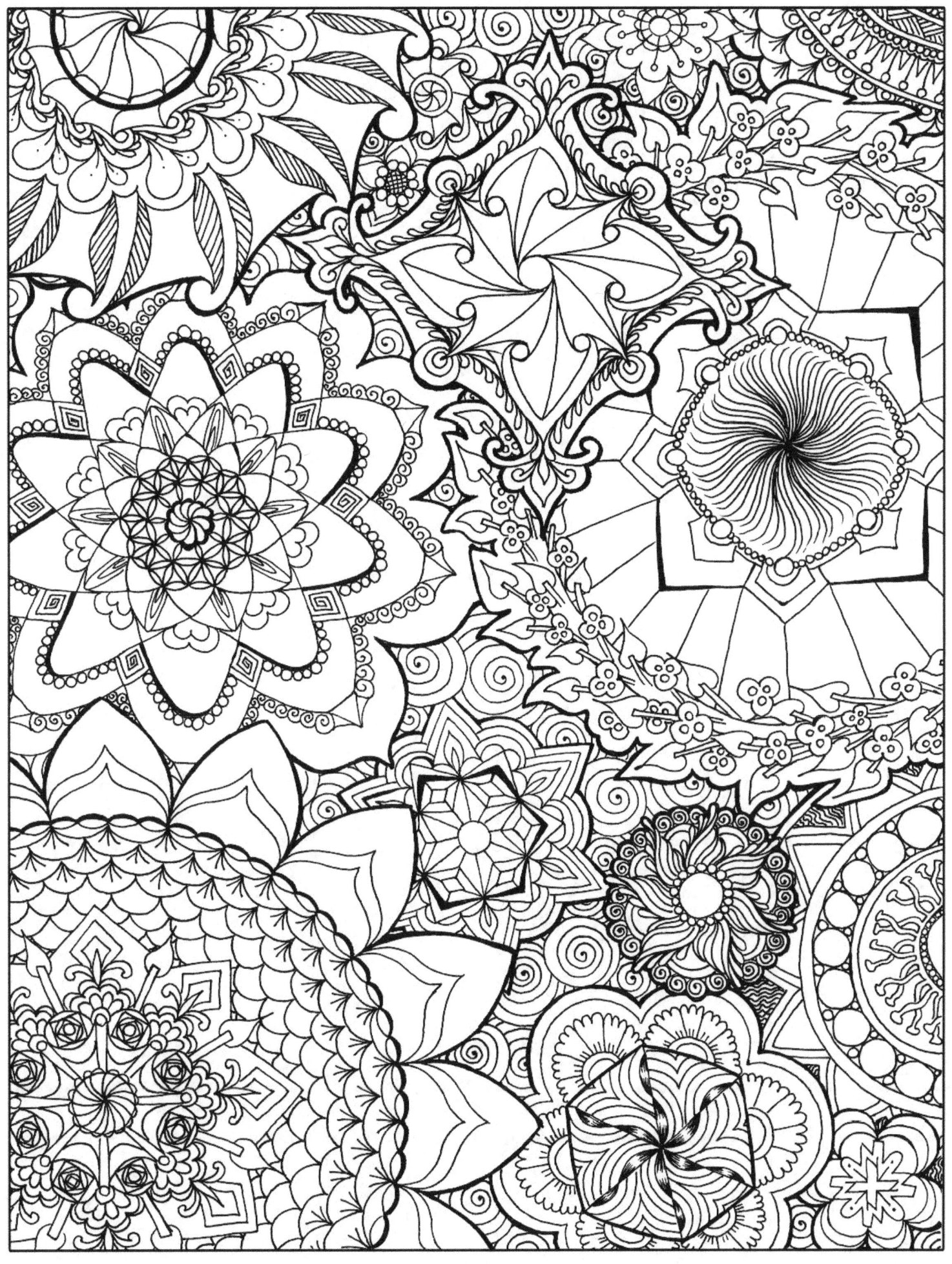

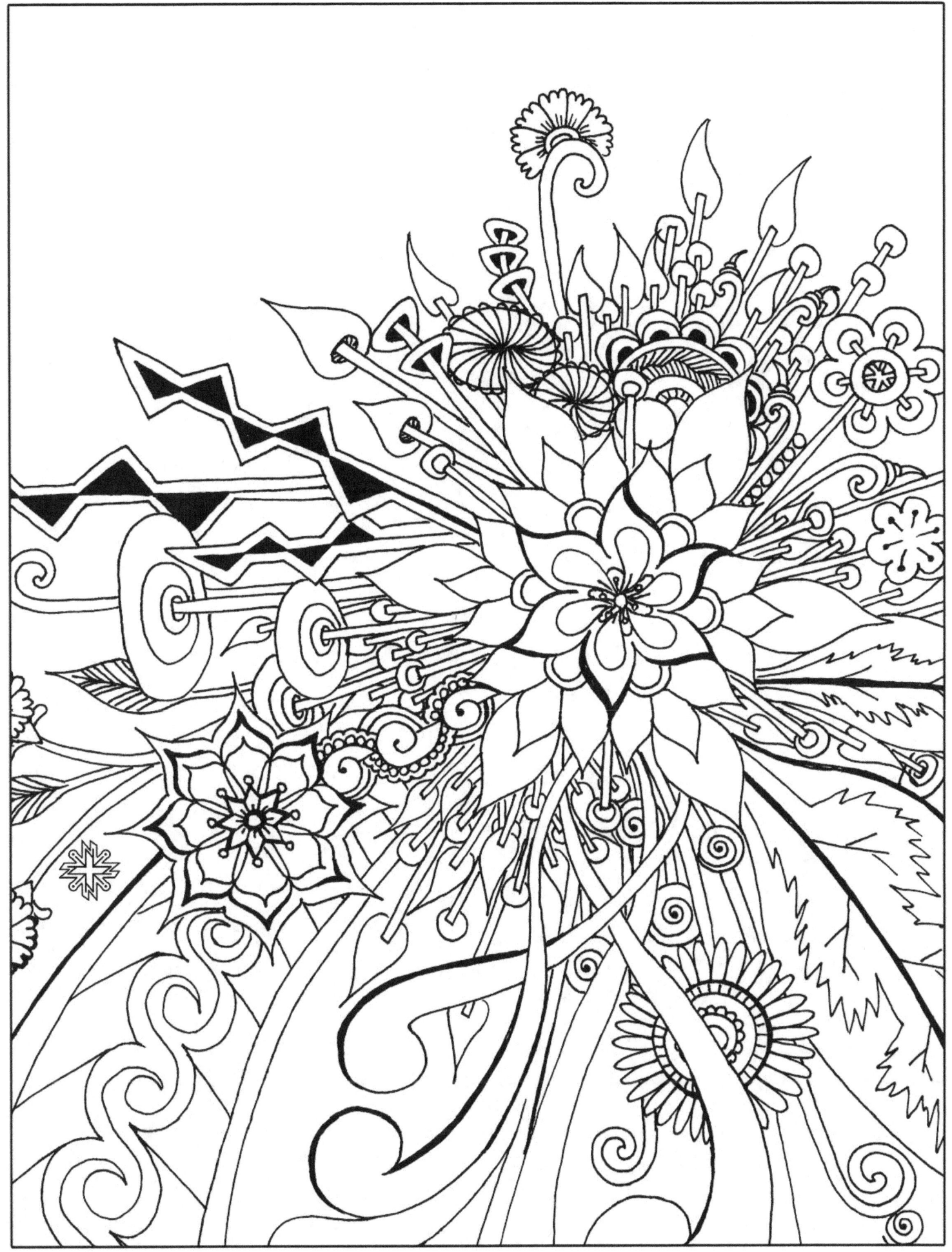

Chapter 6
Jenny Wei
Taiwan
Facebook : zentanglefun

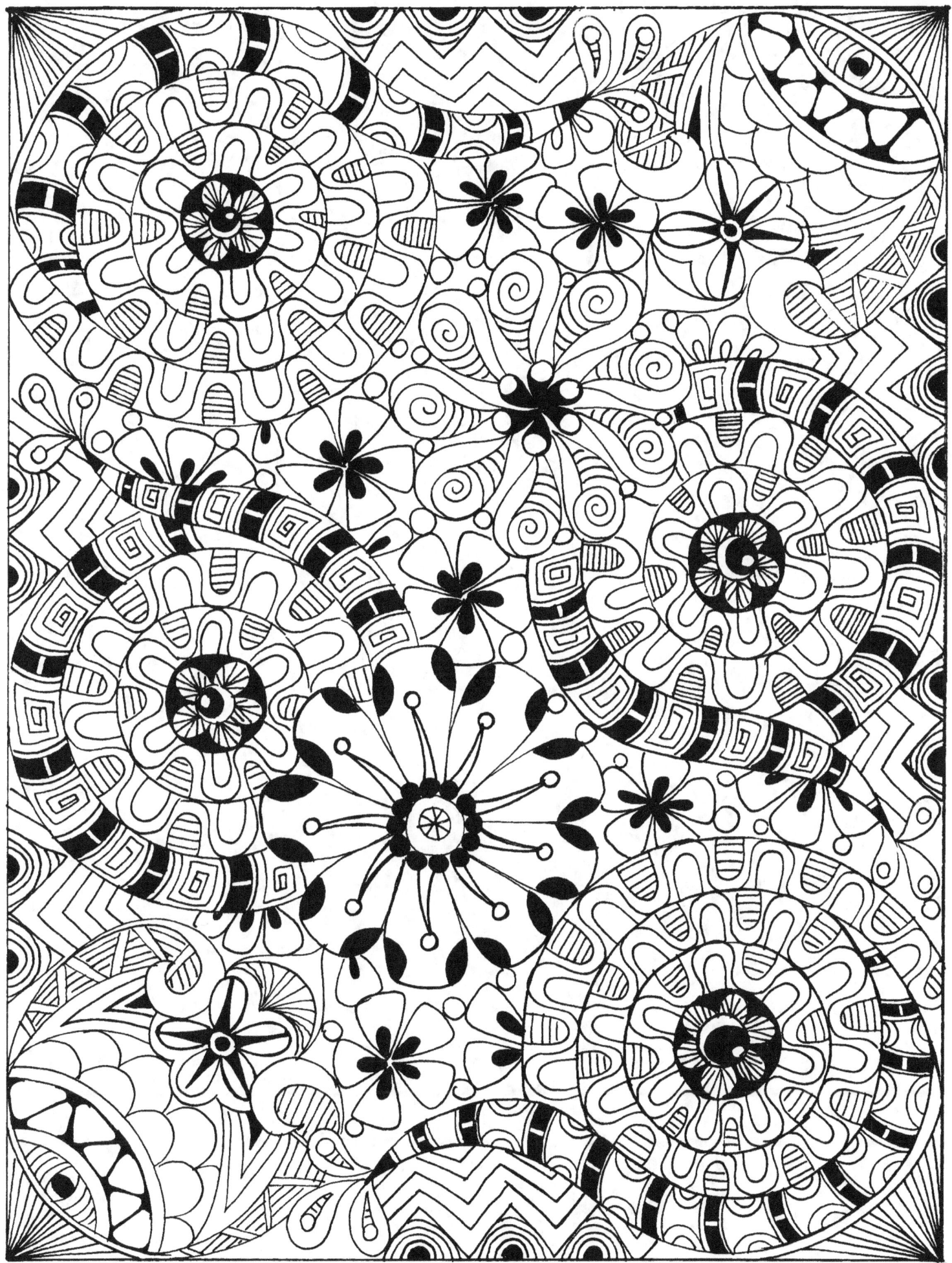

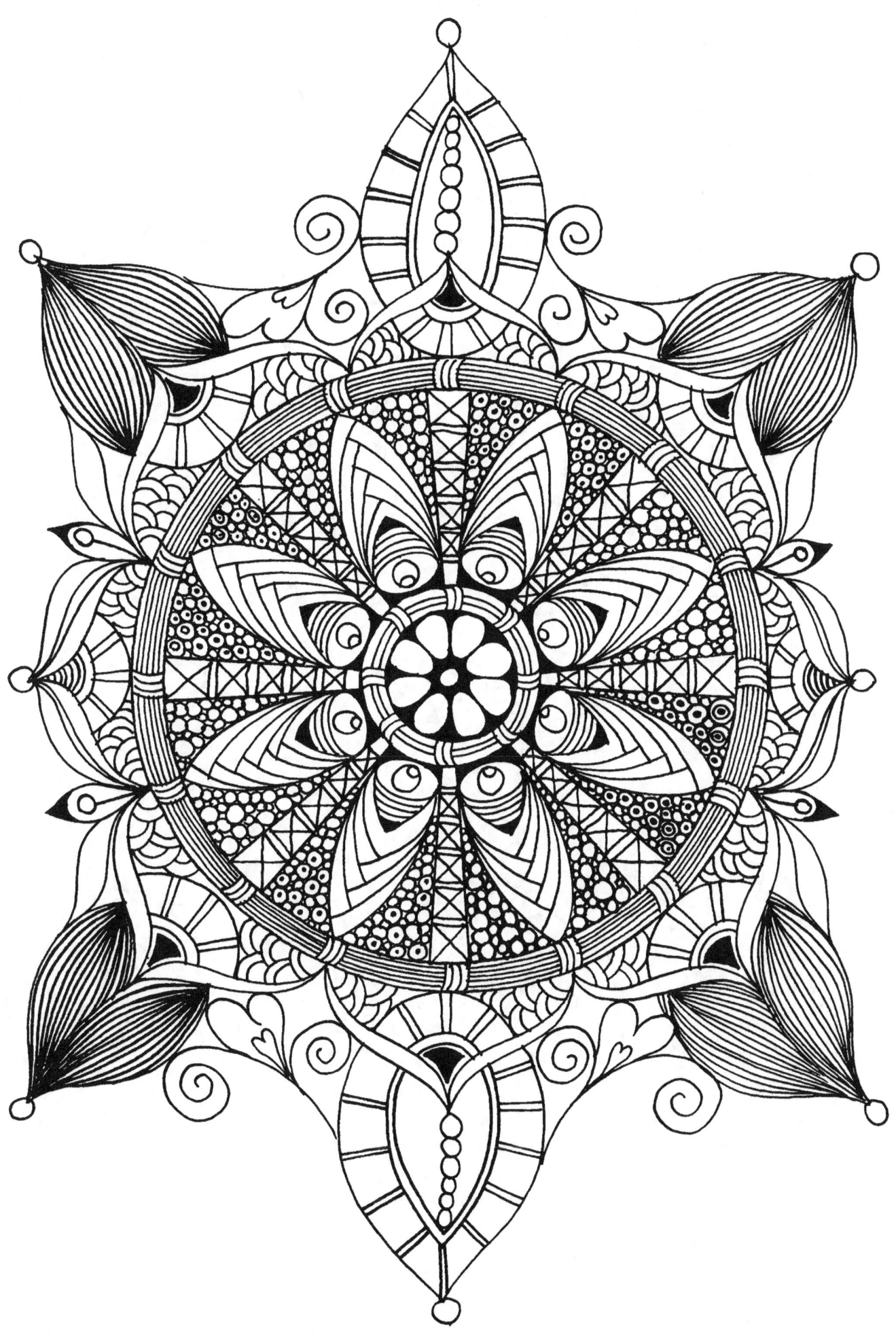

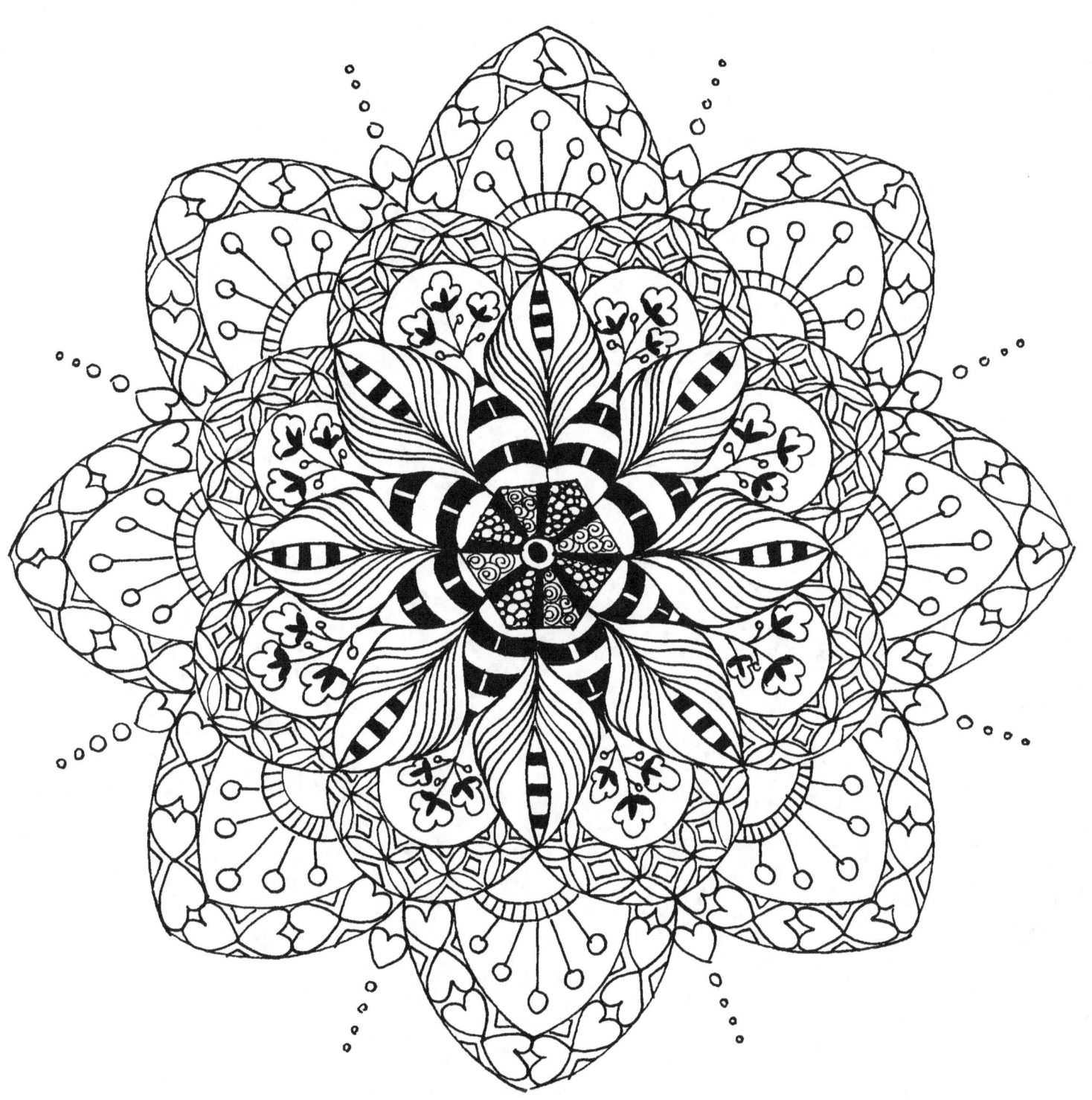

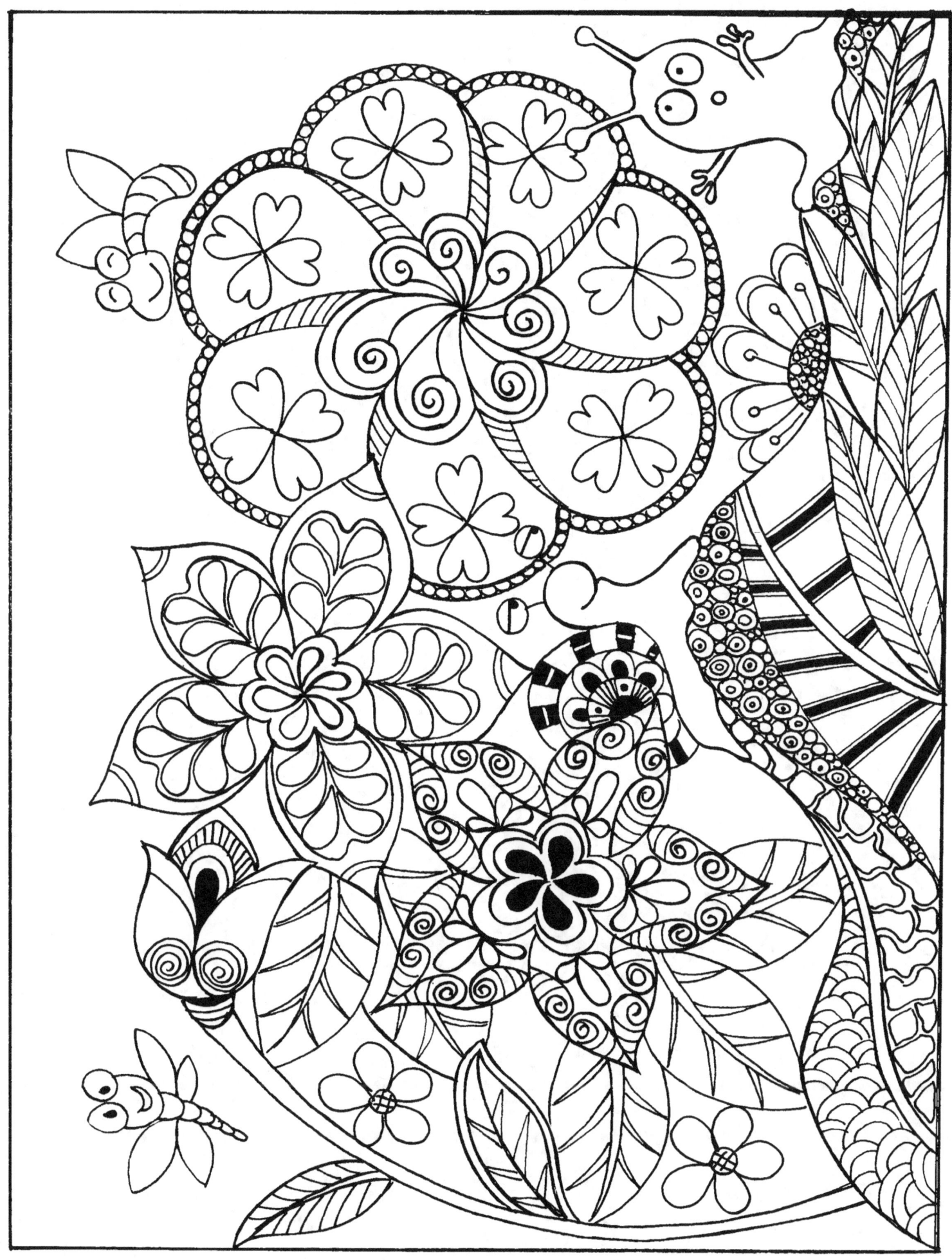

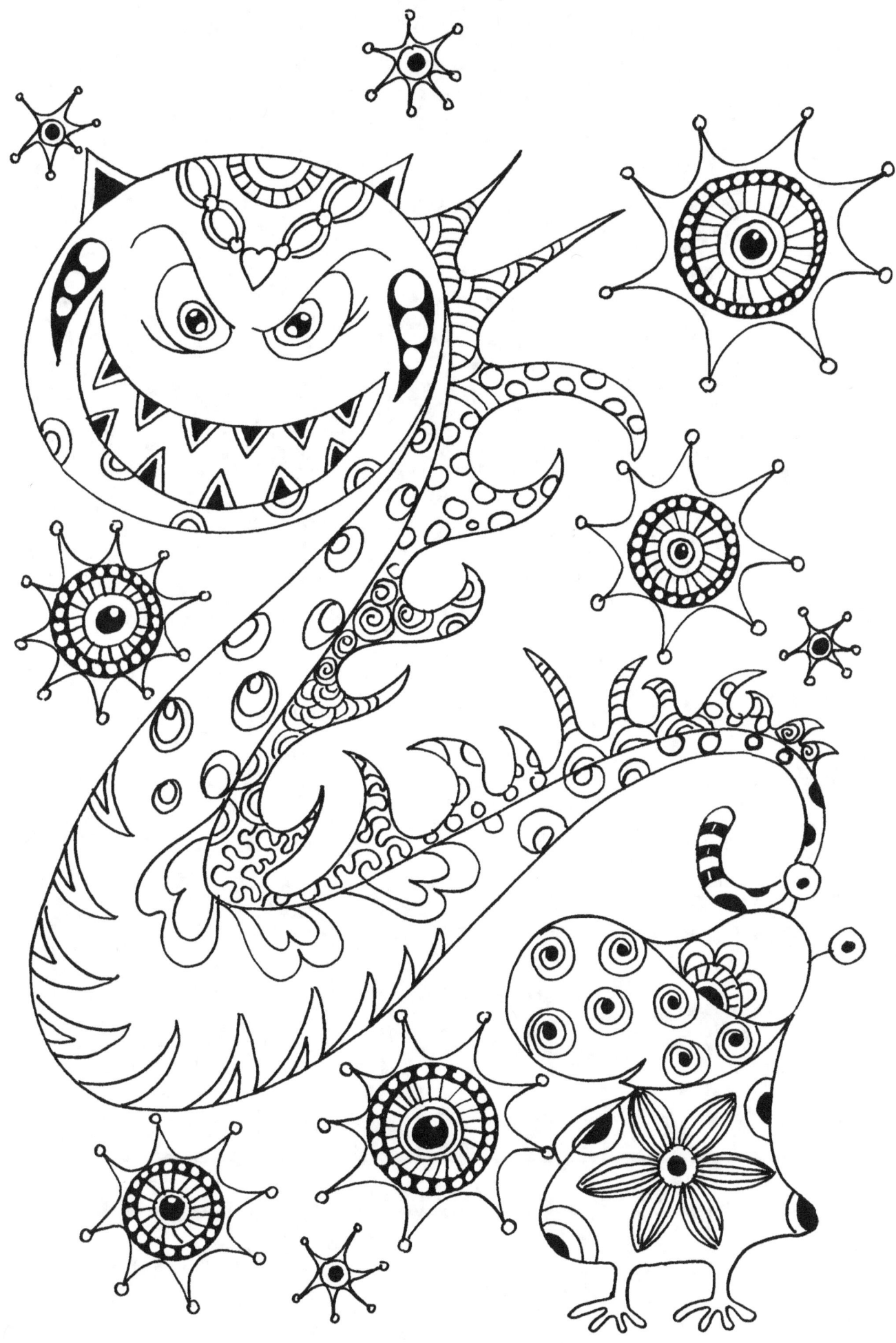

Chapter 7
Mr. End
Taiwan
Facebook : GeometryFlow

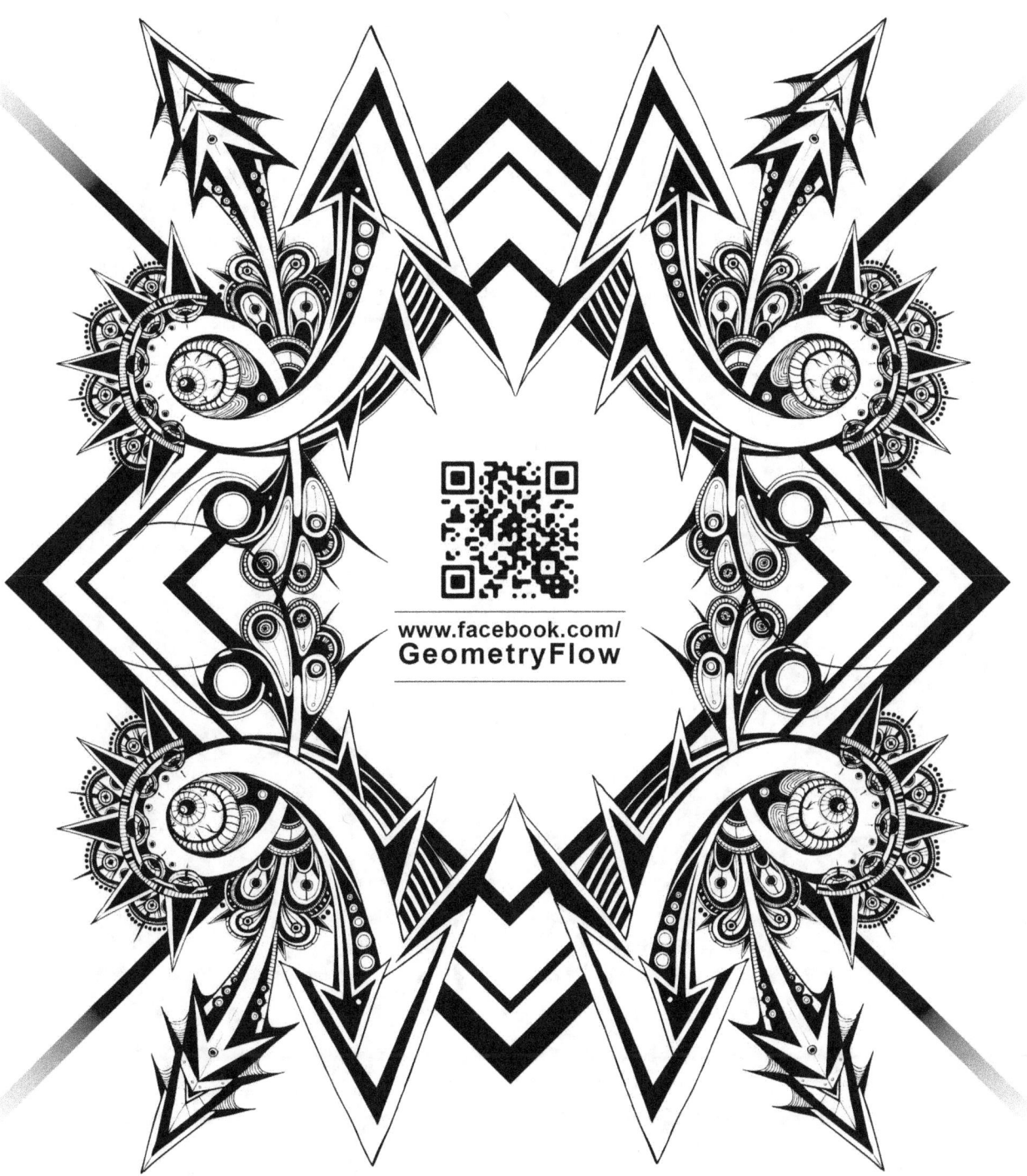

www.facebook.com/
GeometryFlow

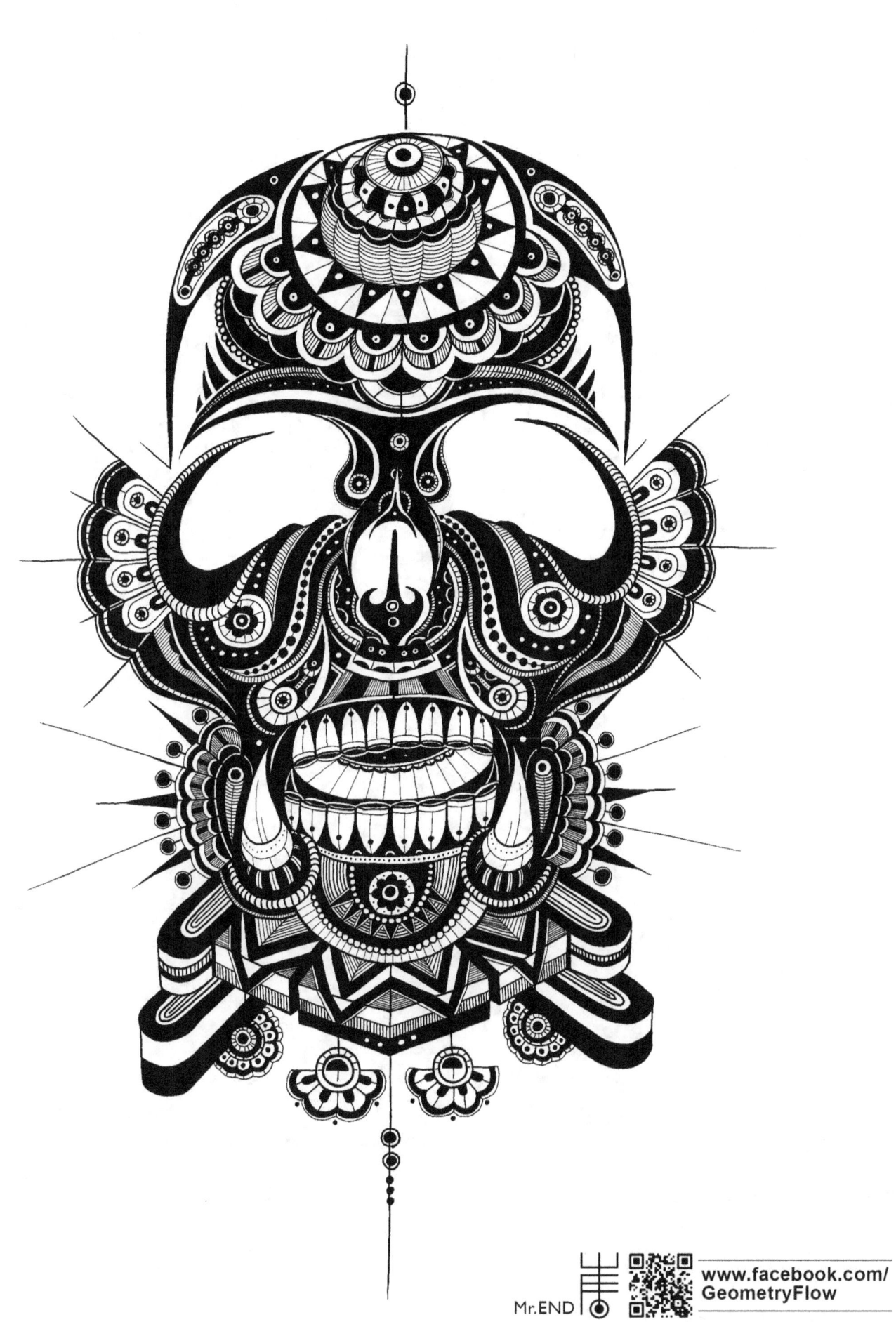

Mr.END www.facebook.com/GeometryFlow

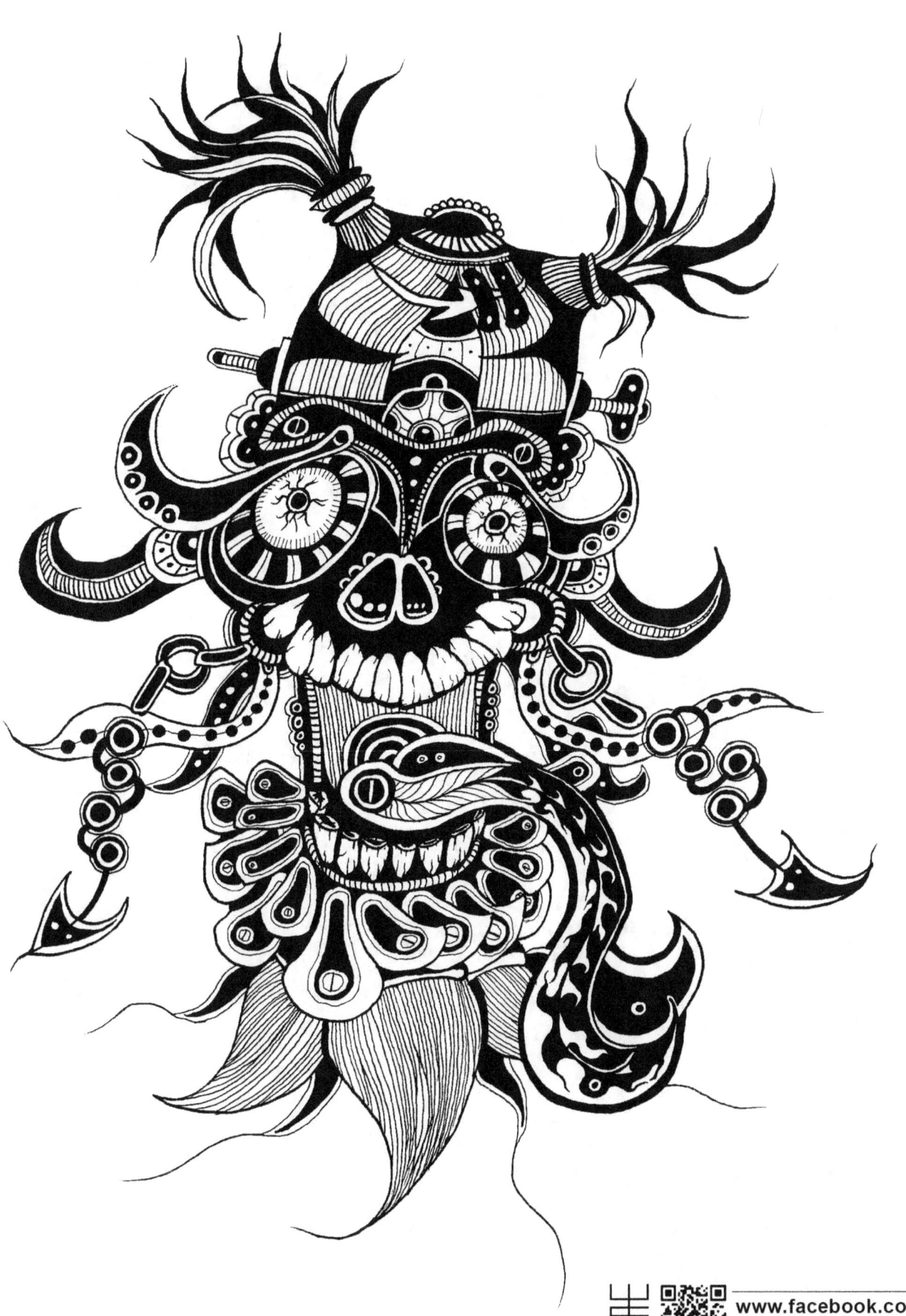

www.facebook.com/GeometryFlow

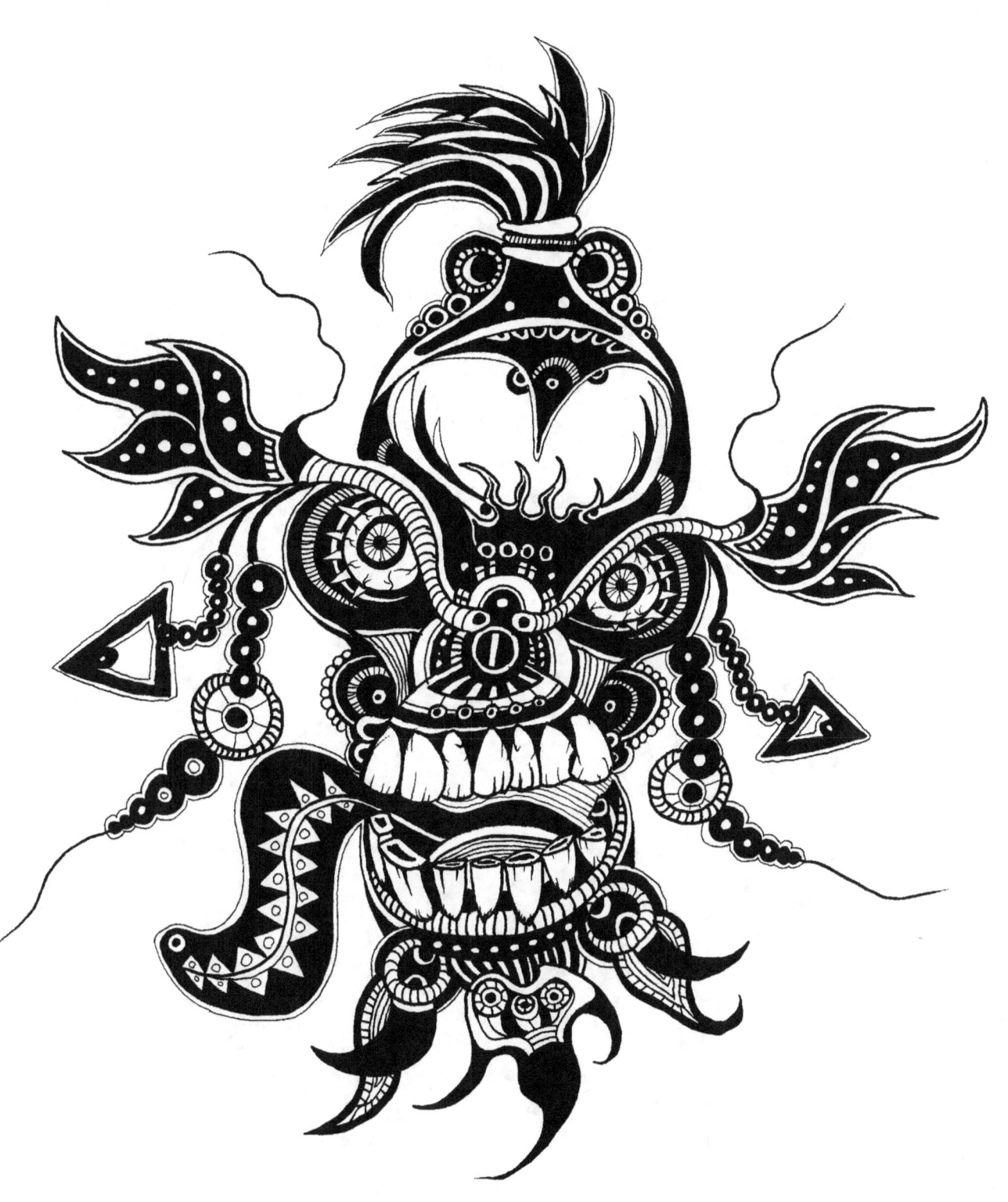

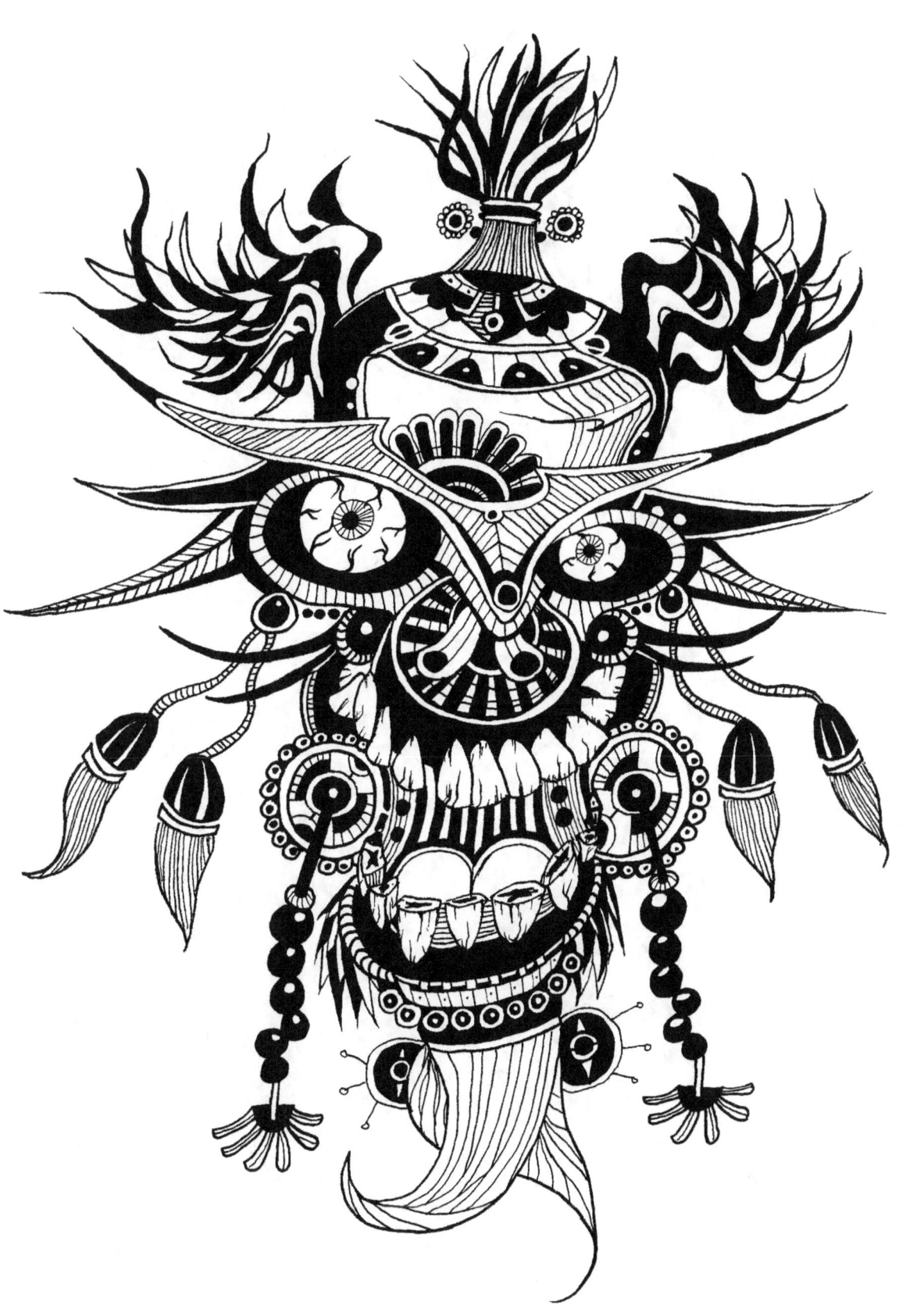

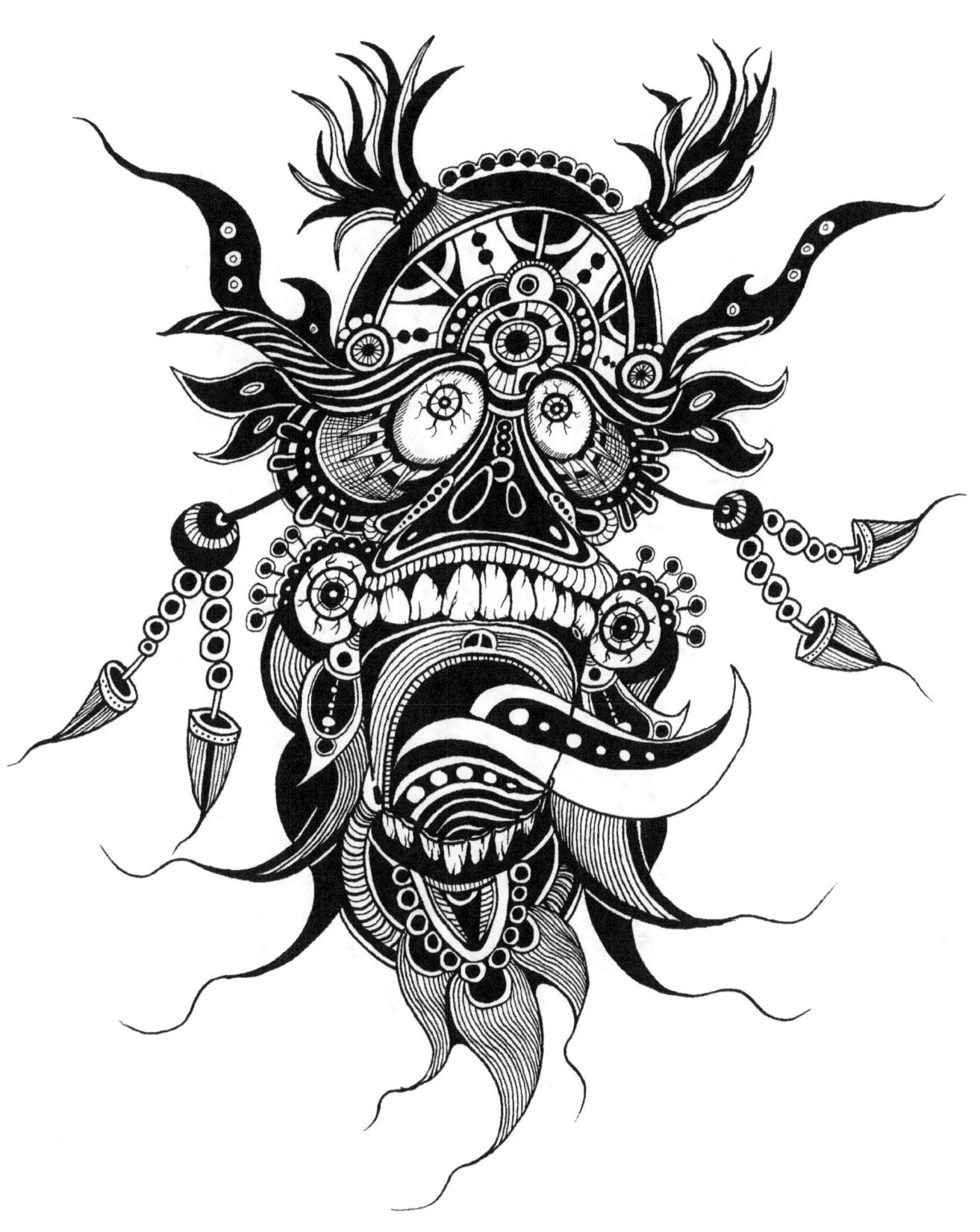

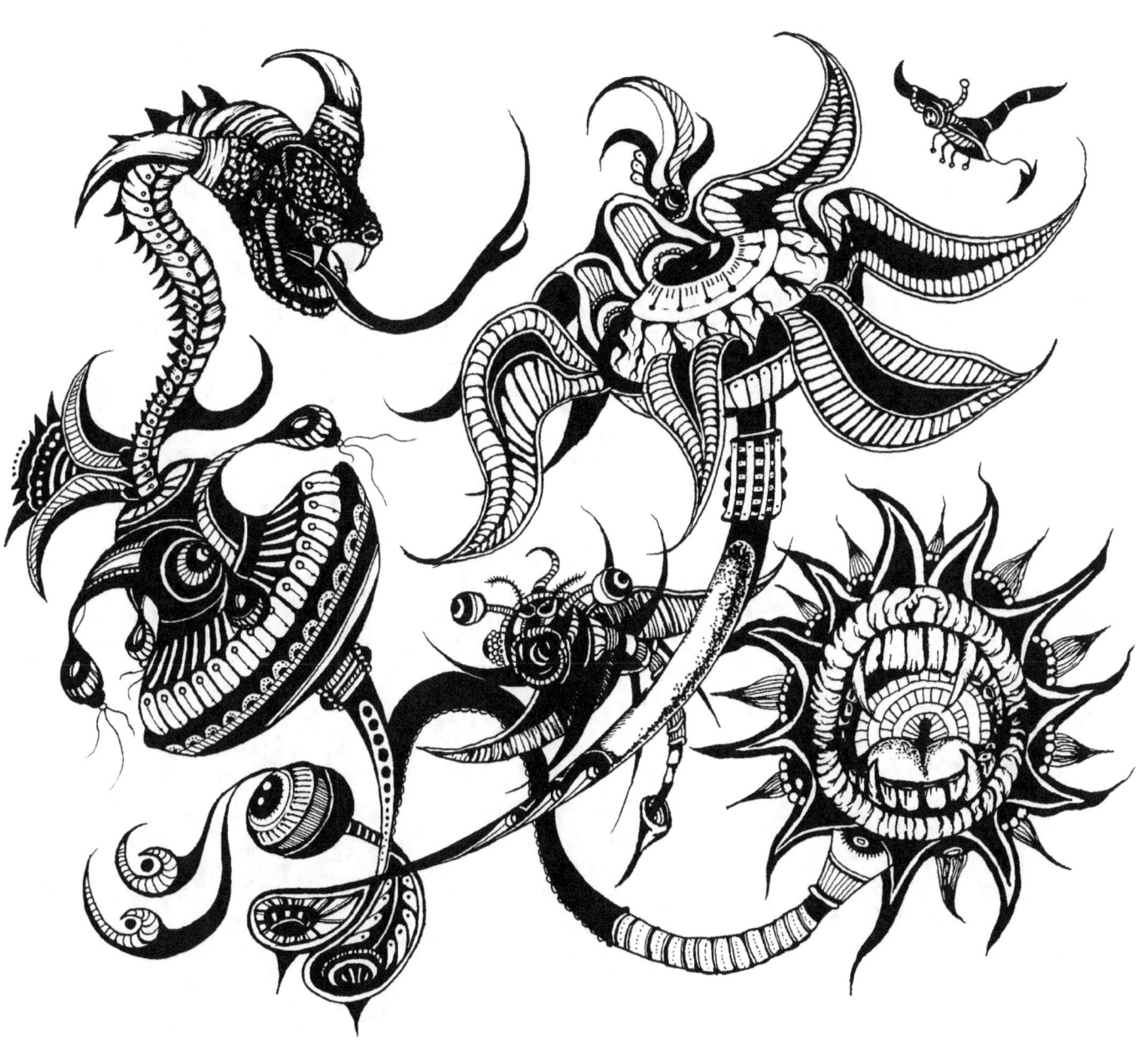

www.facebook.com/GeometryFlow

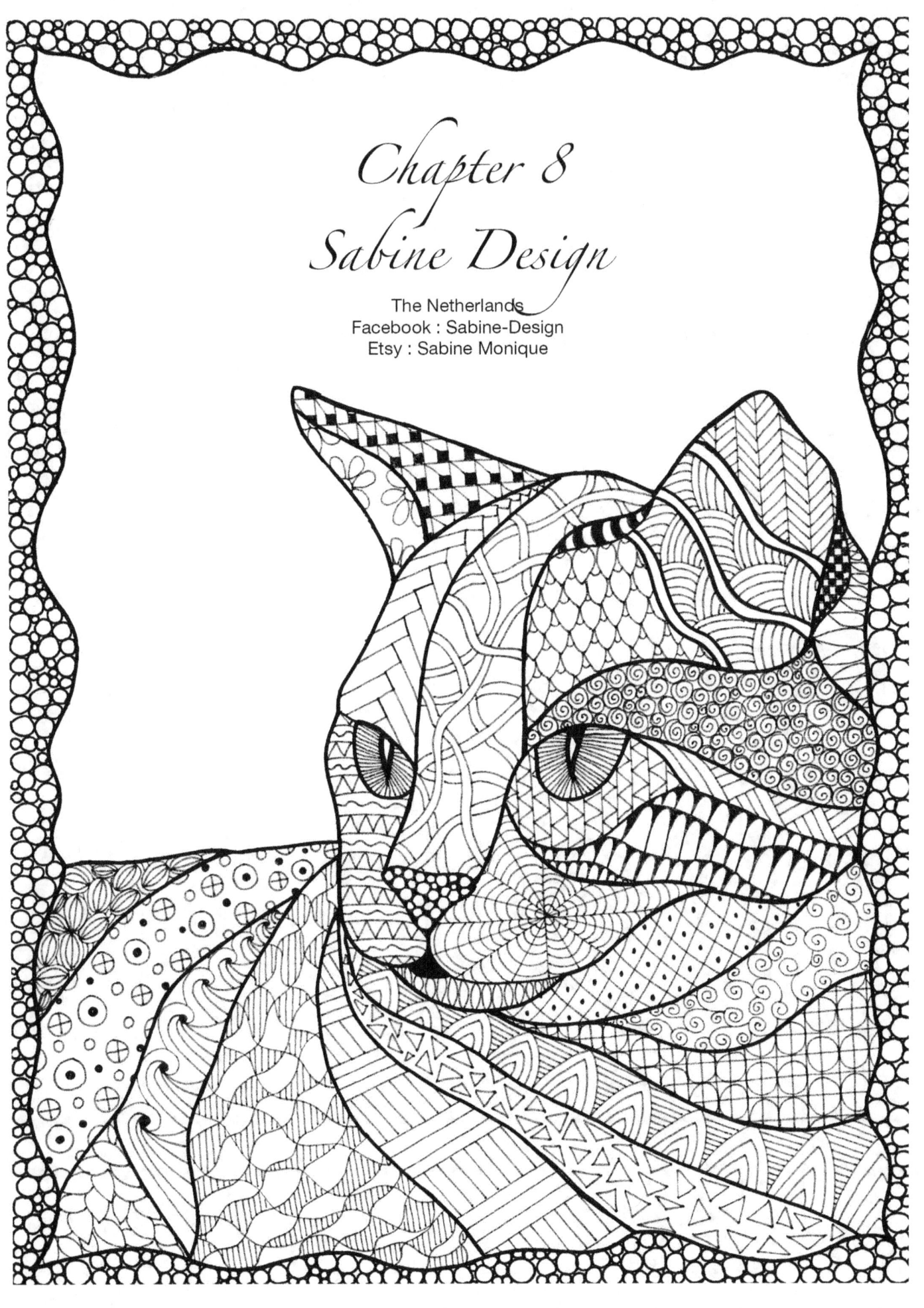

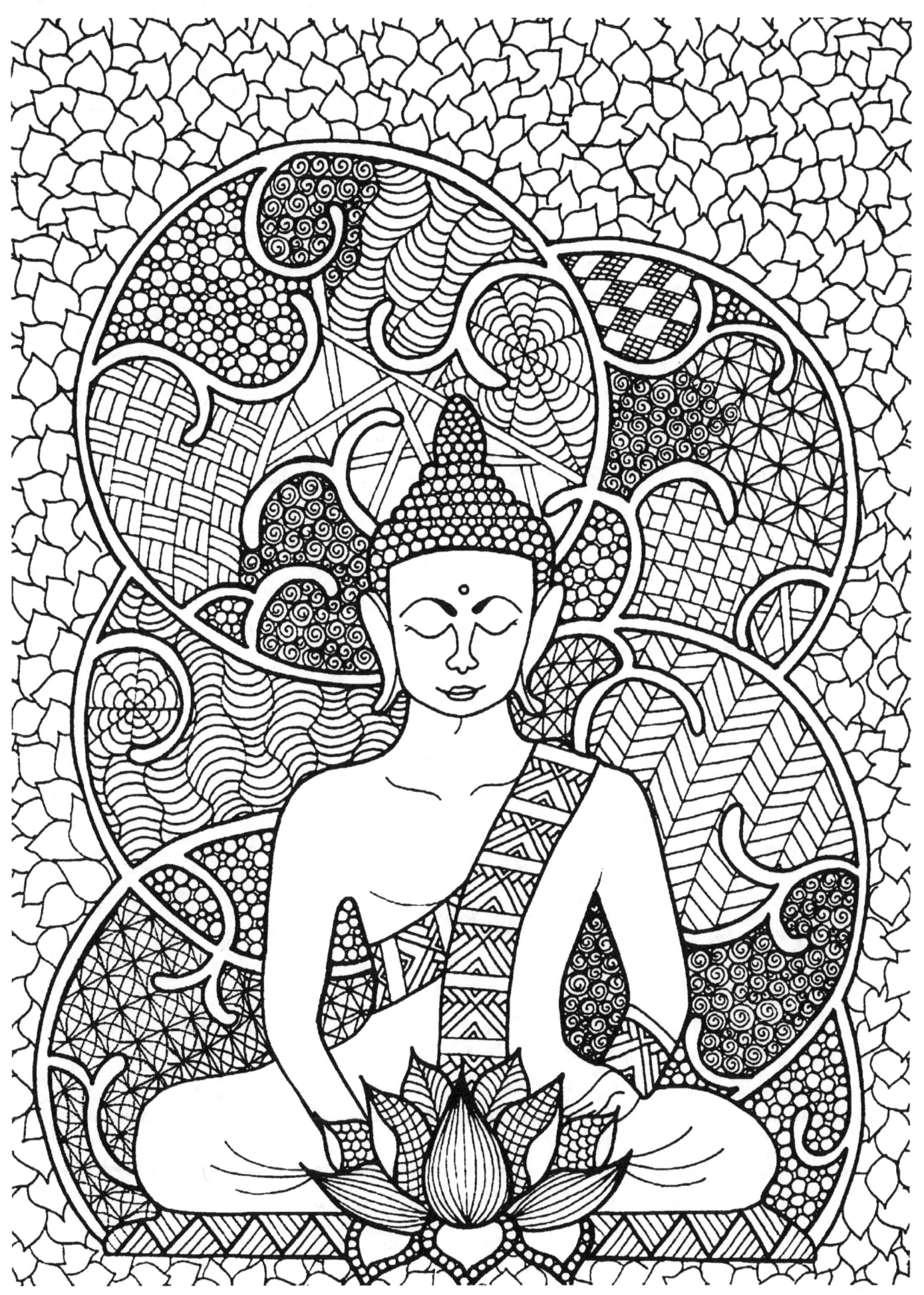

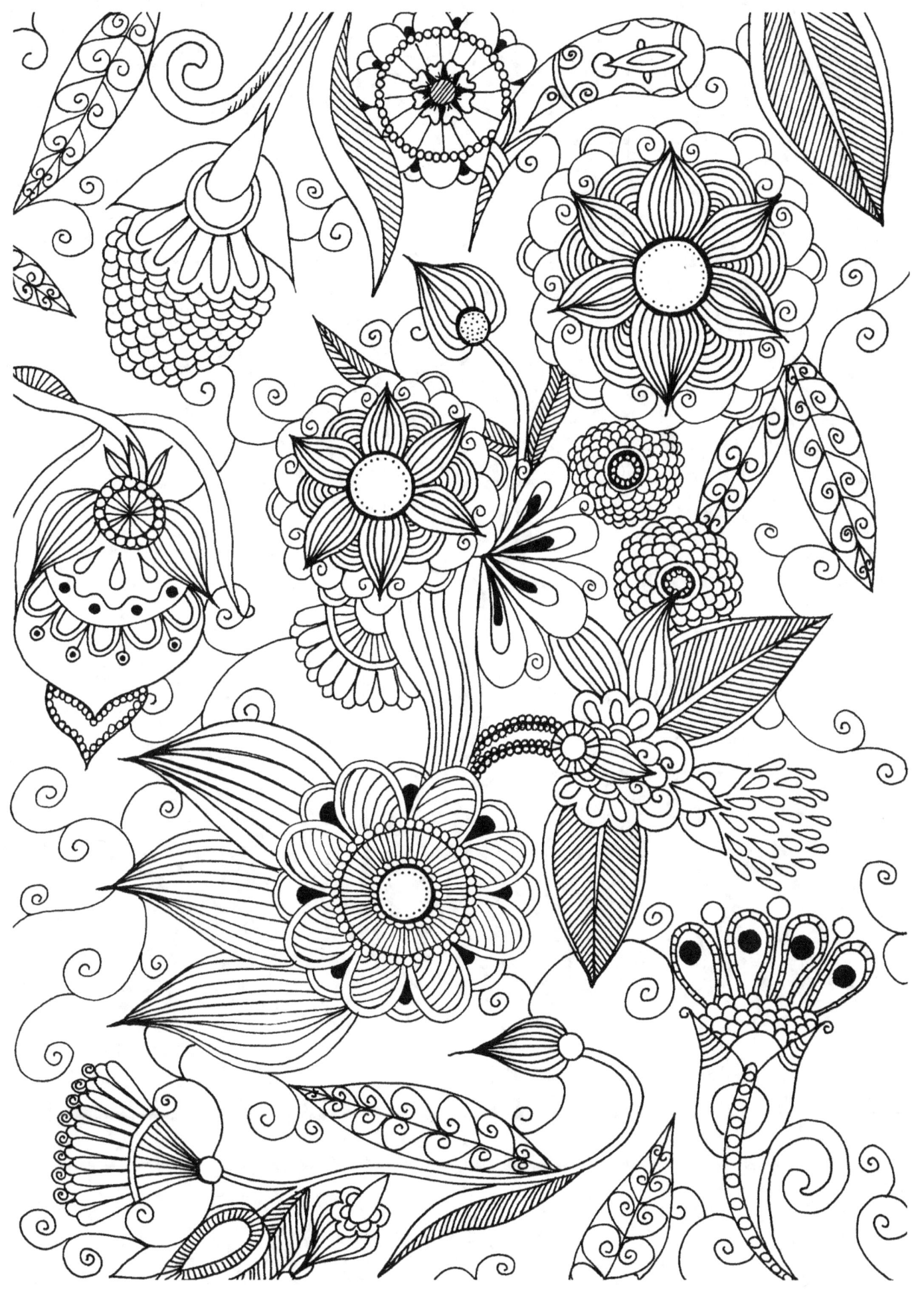

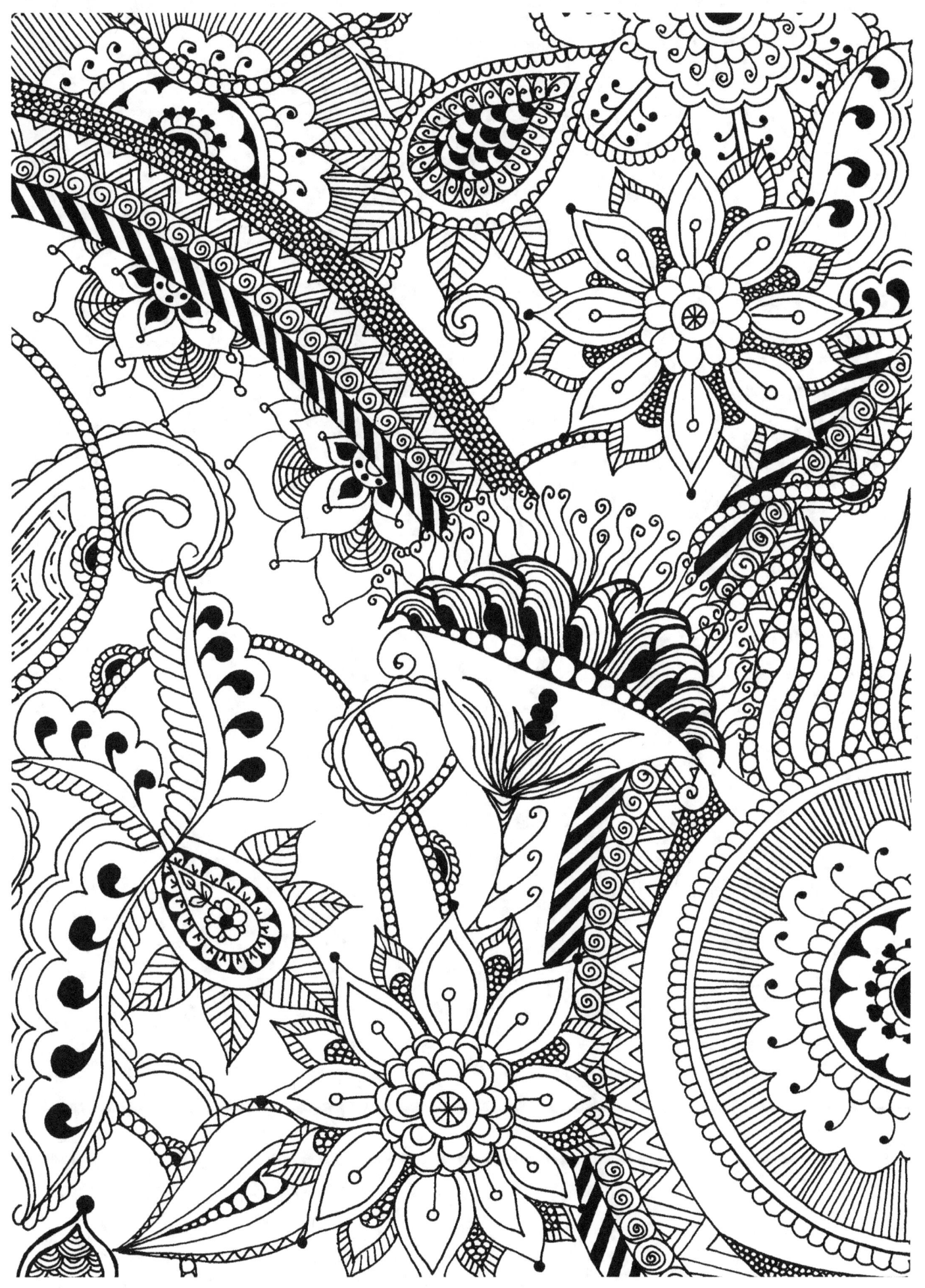

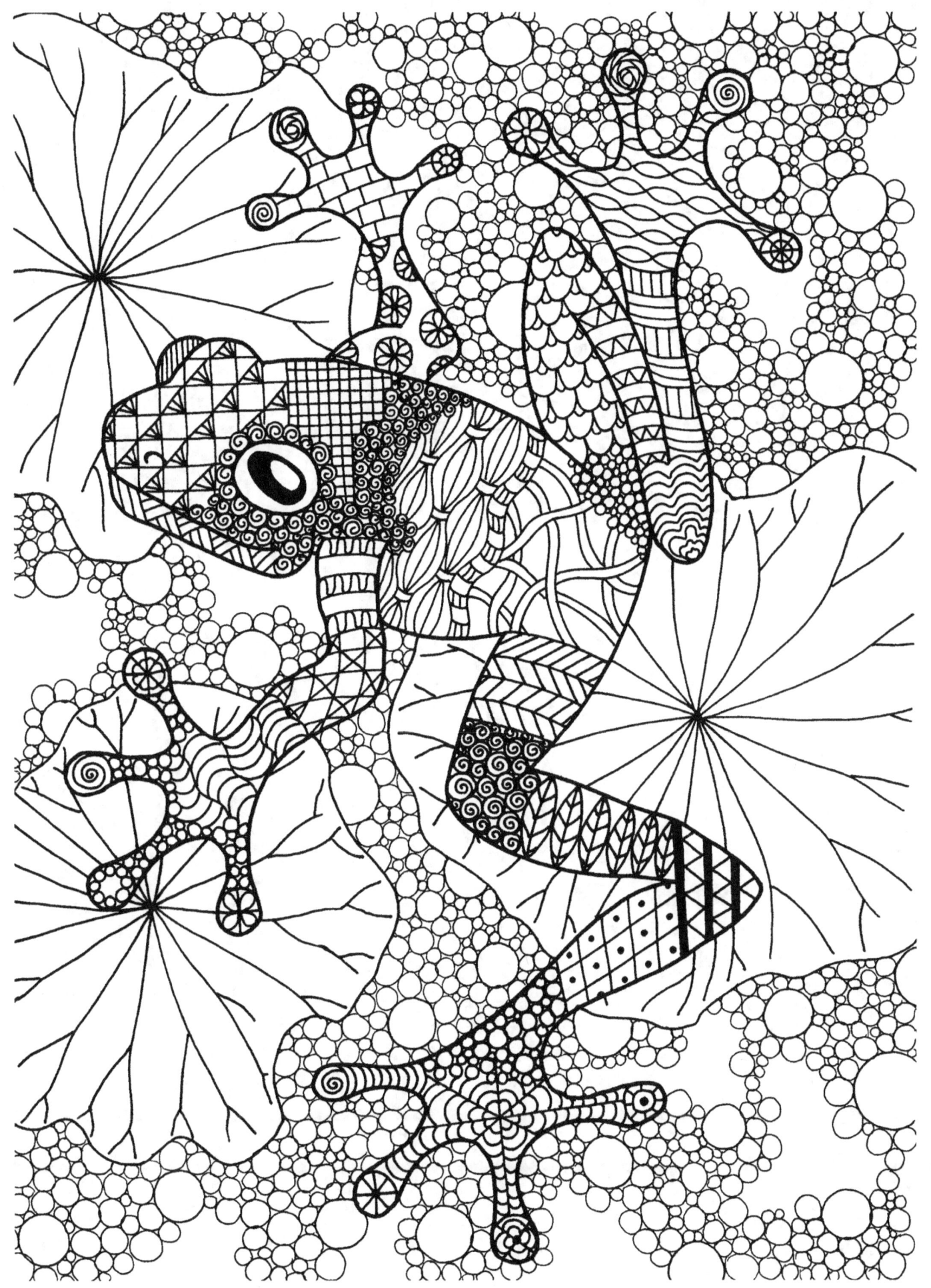

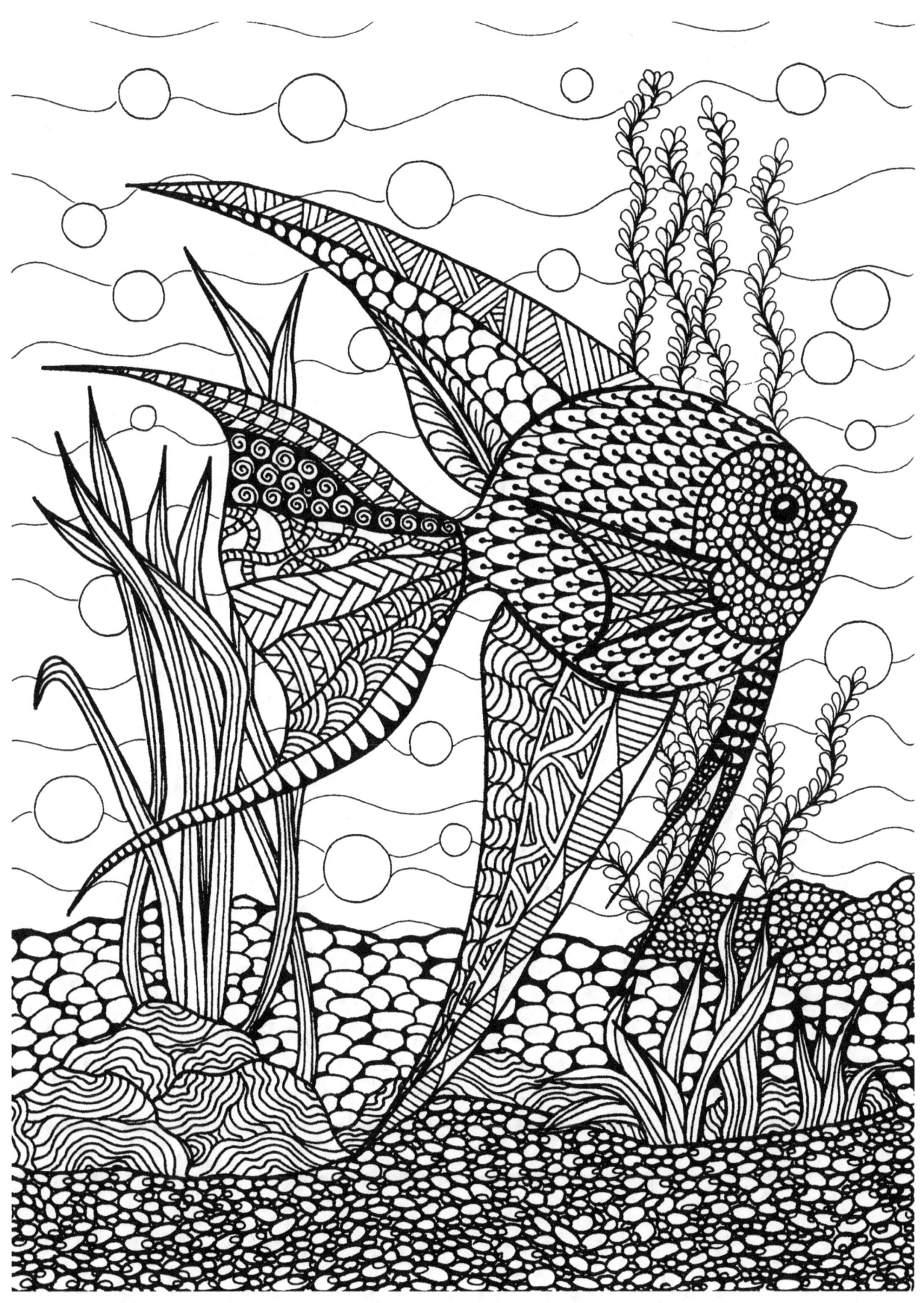

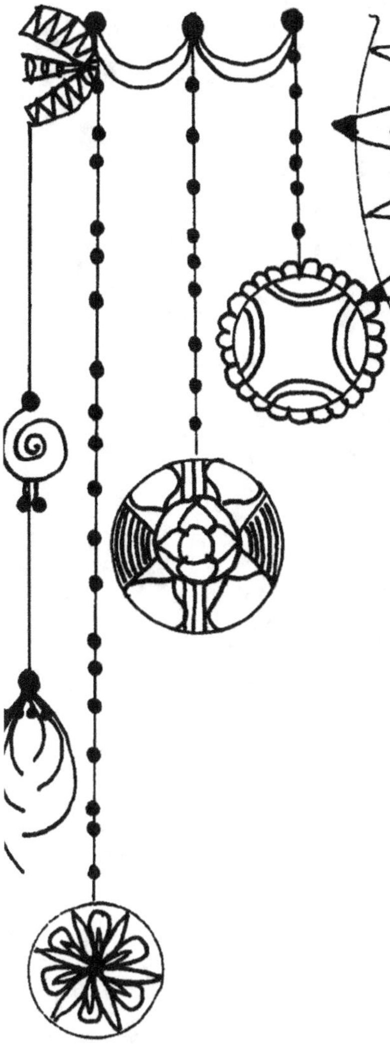

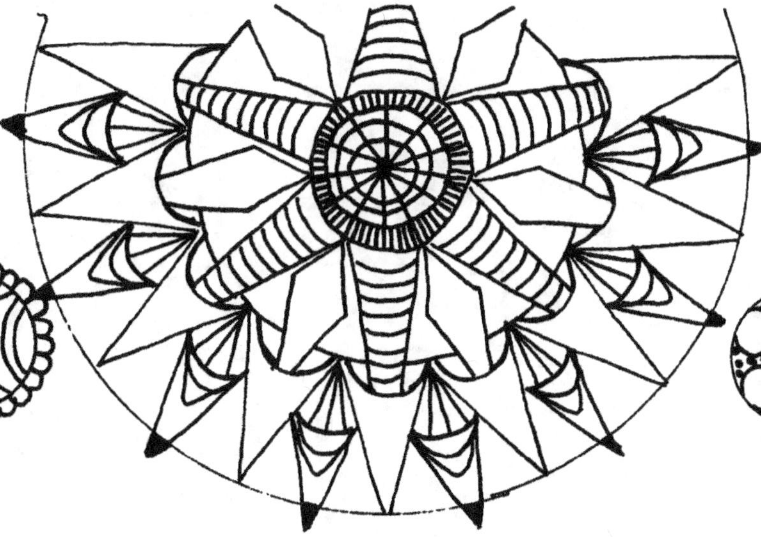

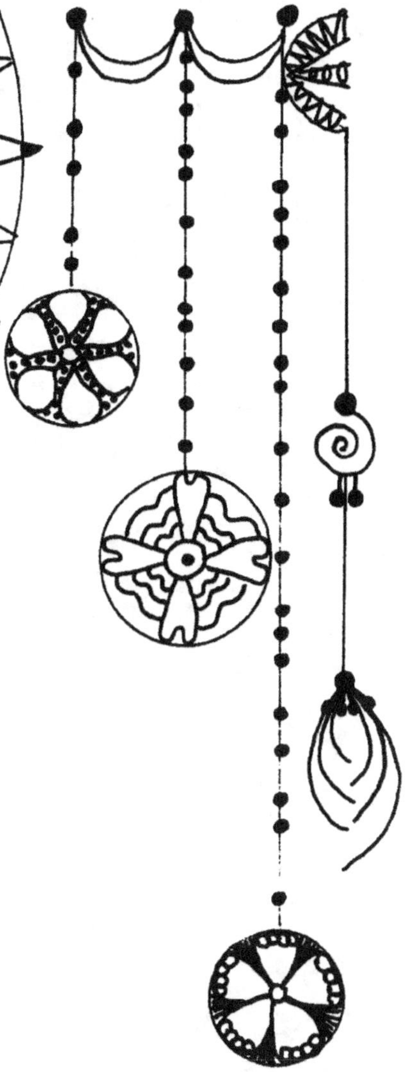

Chapter 9
Diane Pick-Ross

USA
Facebook : Doodles-By-Diane

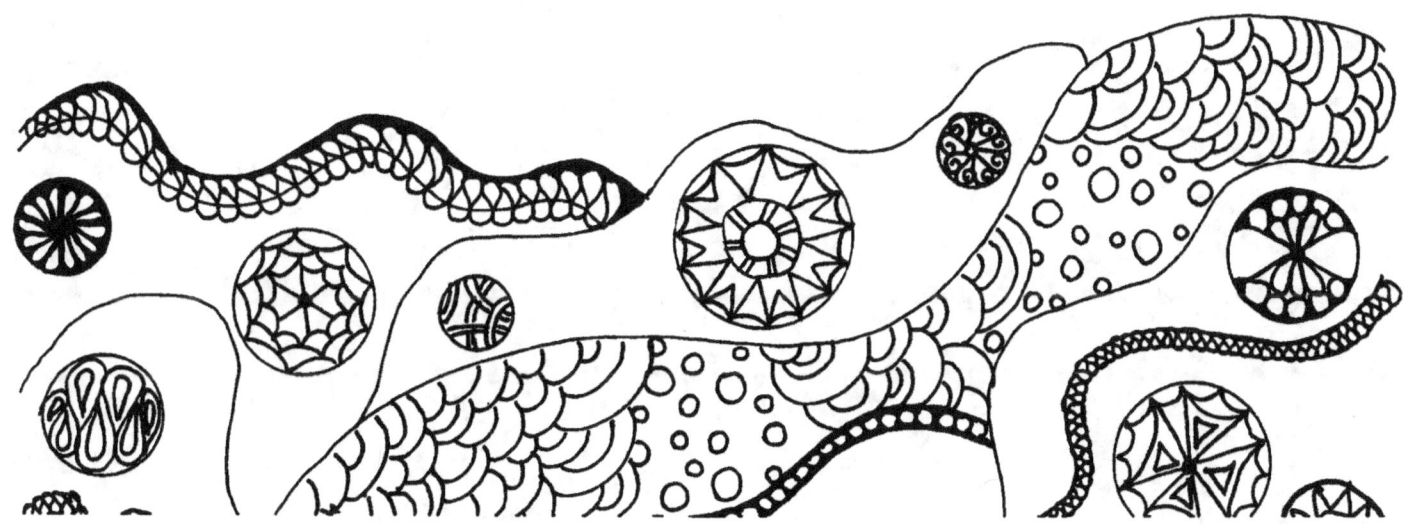

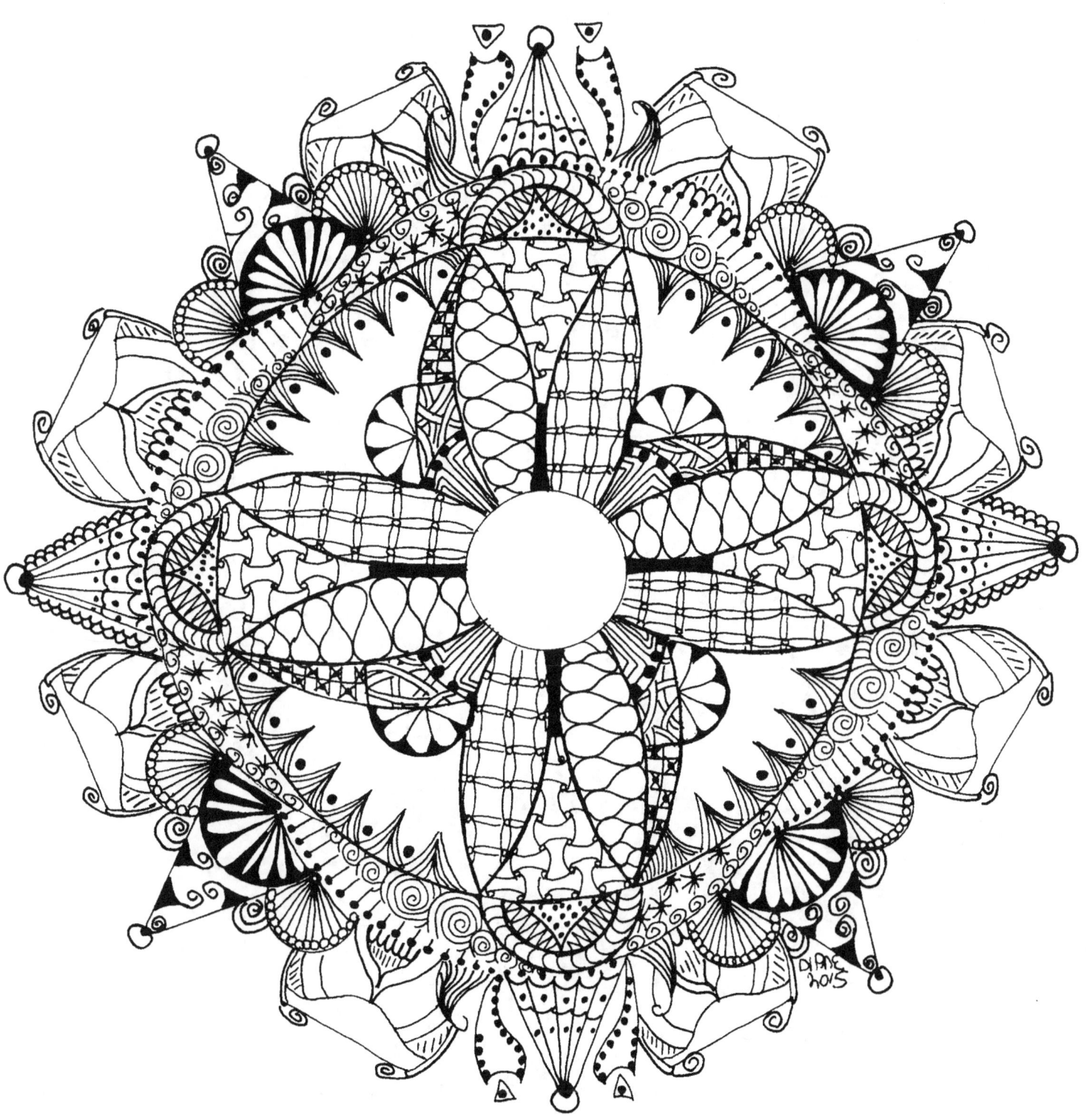

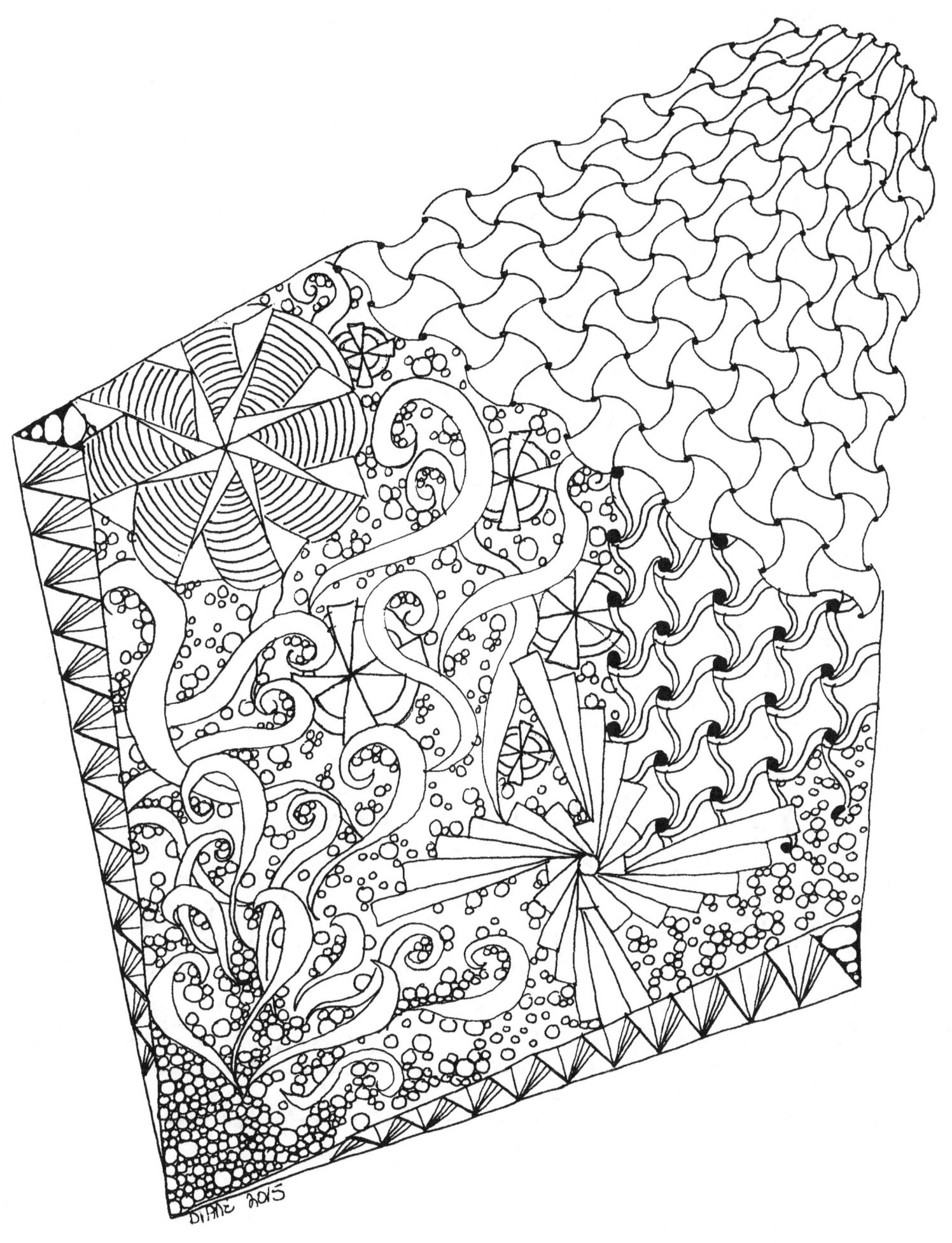

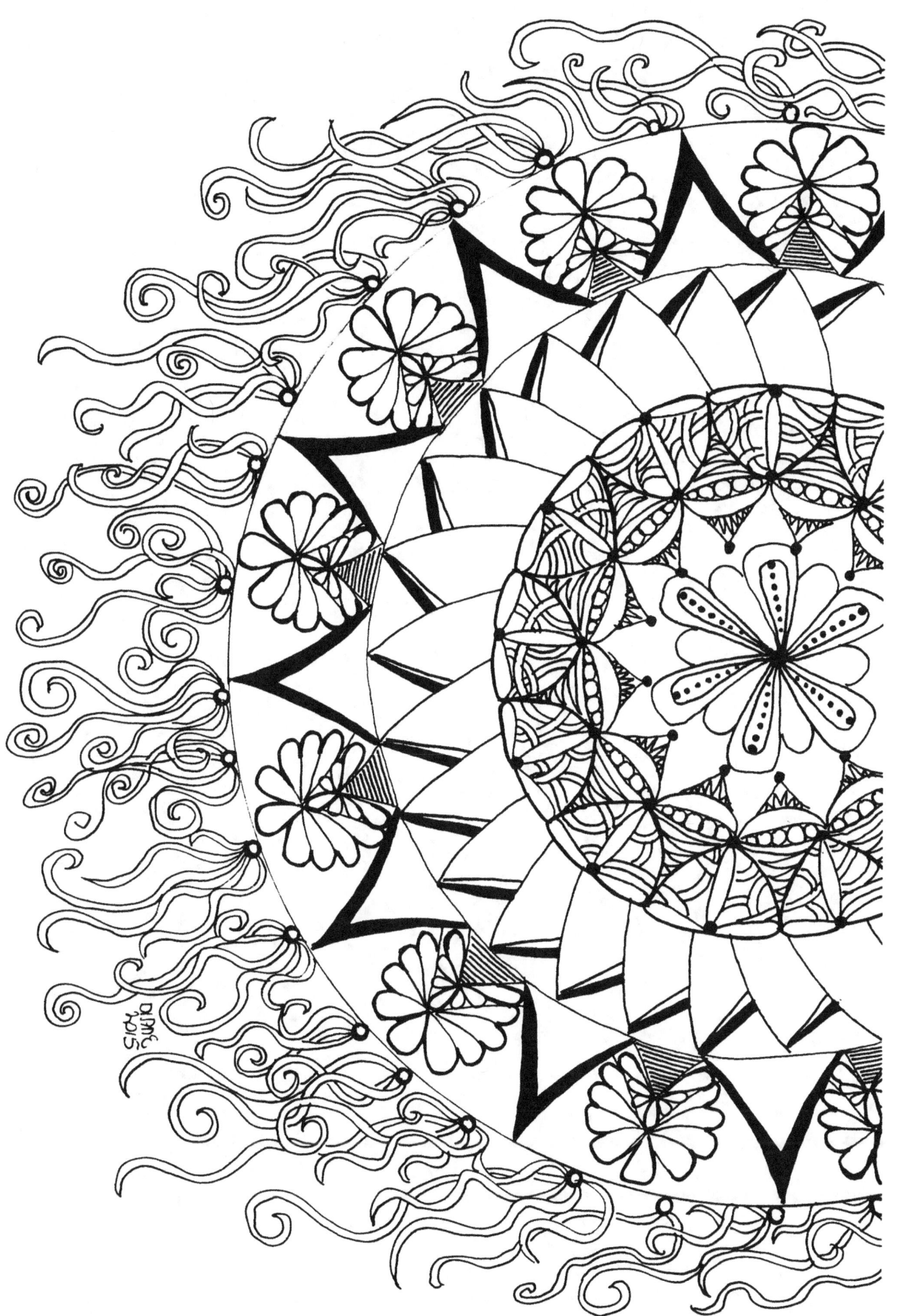

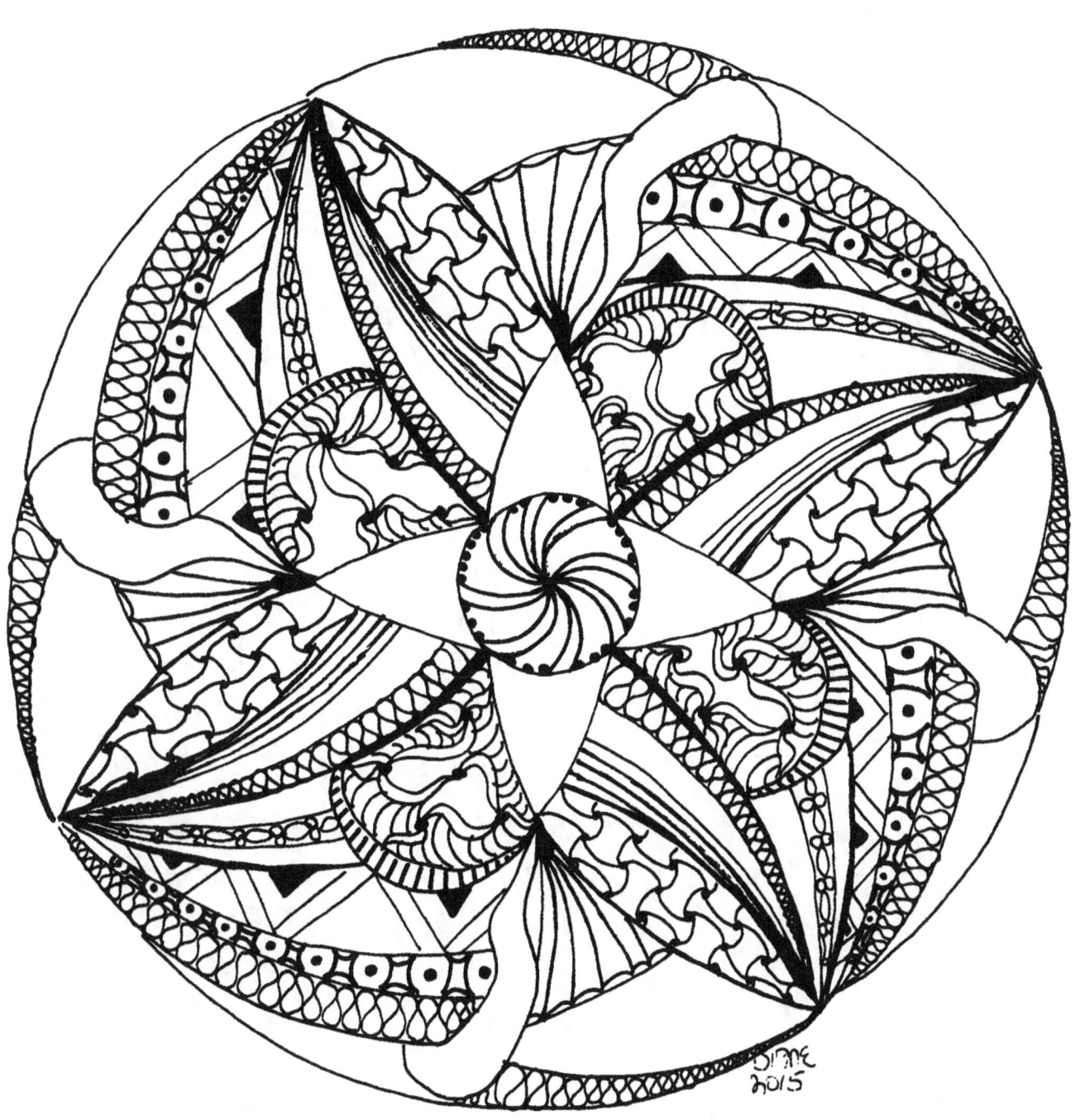

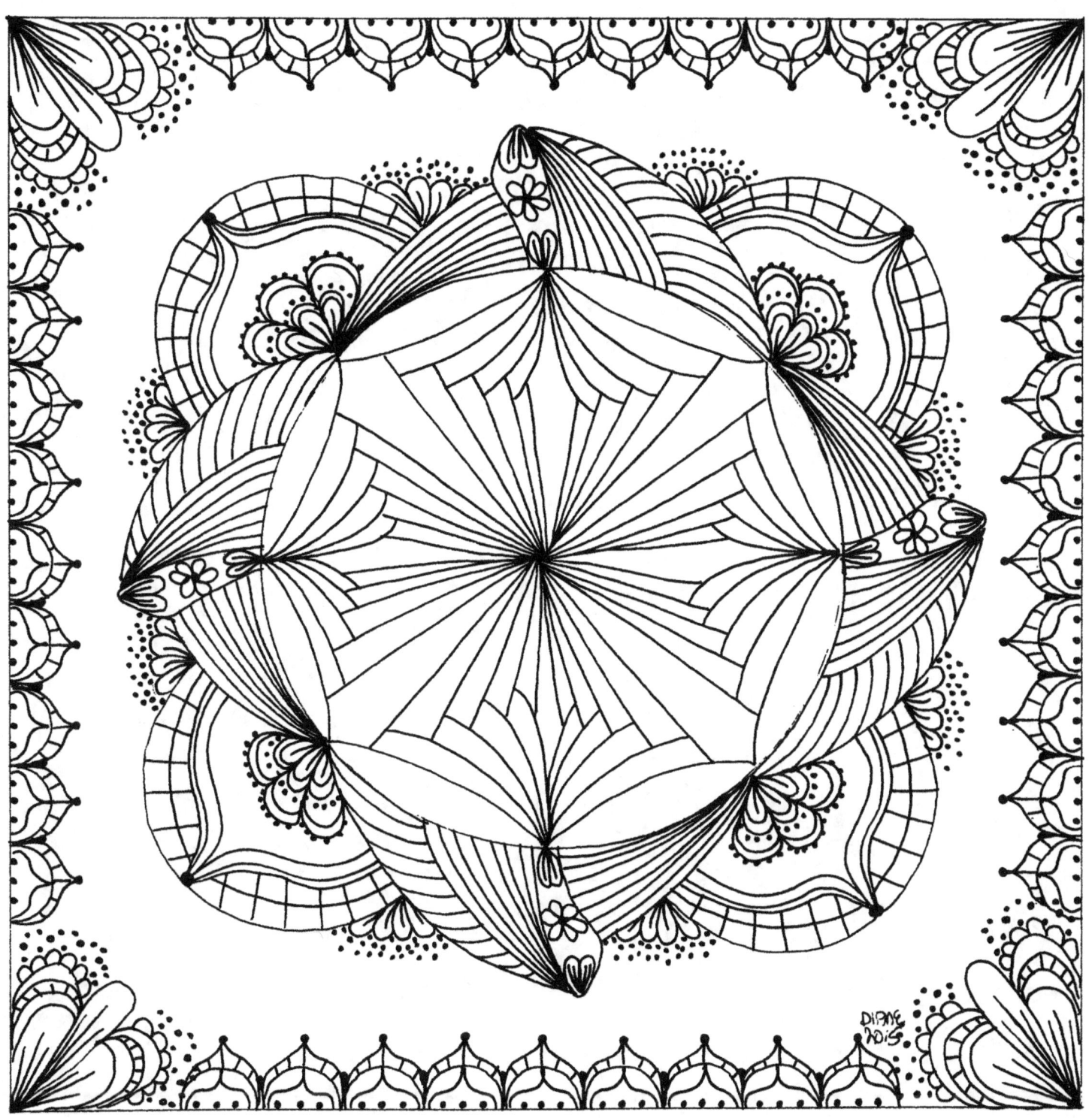

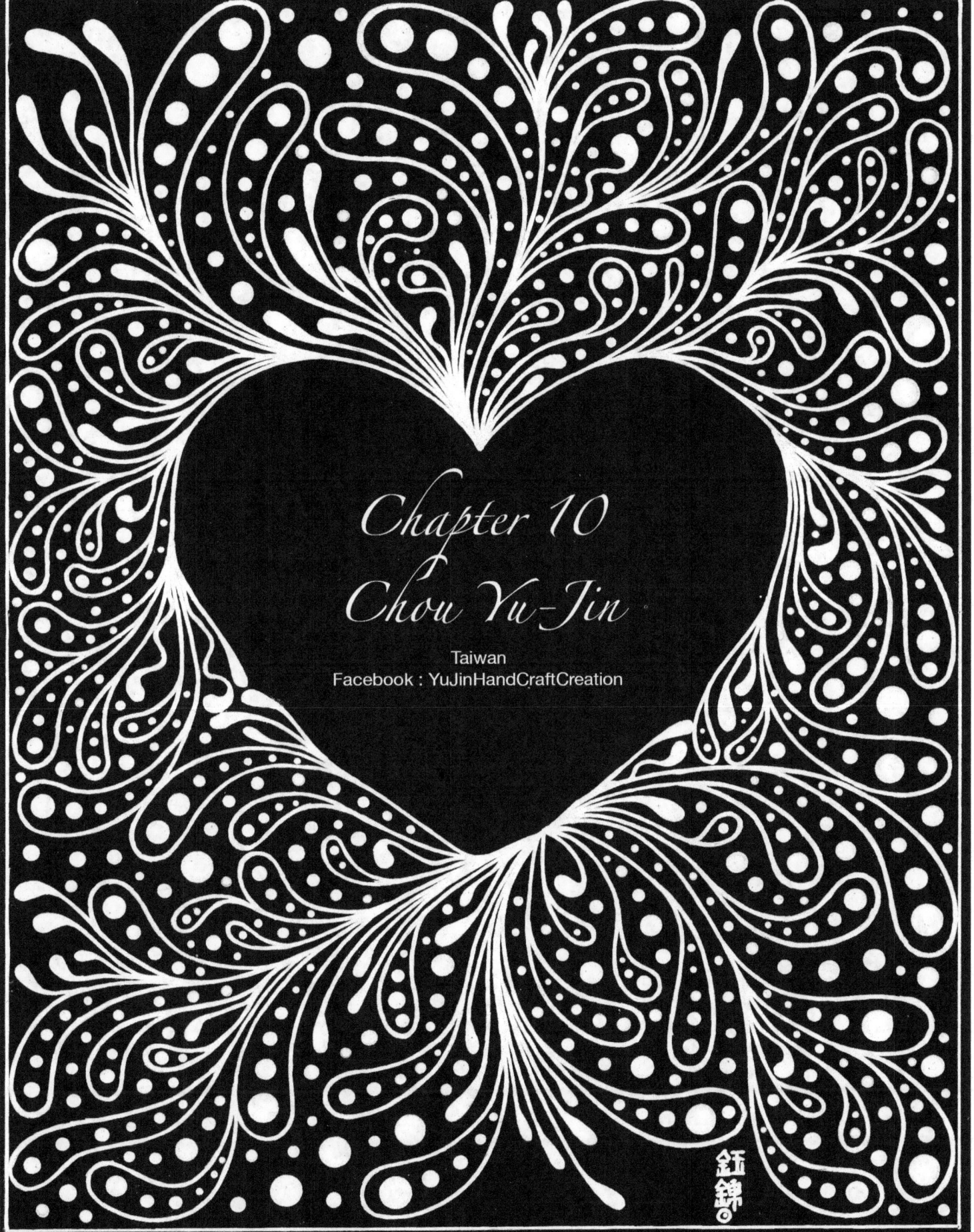

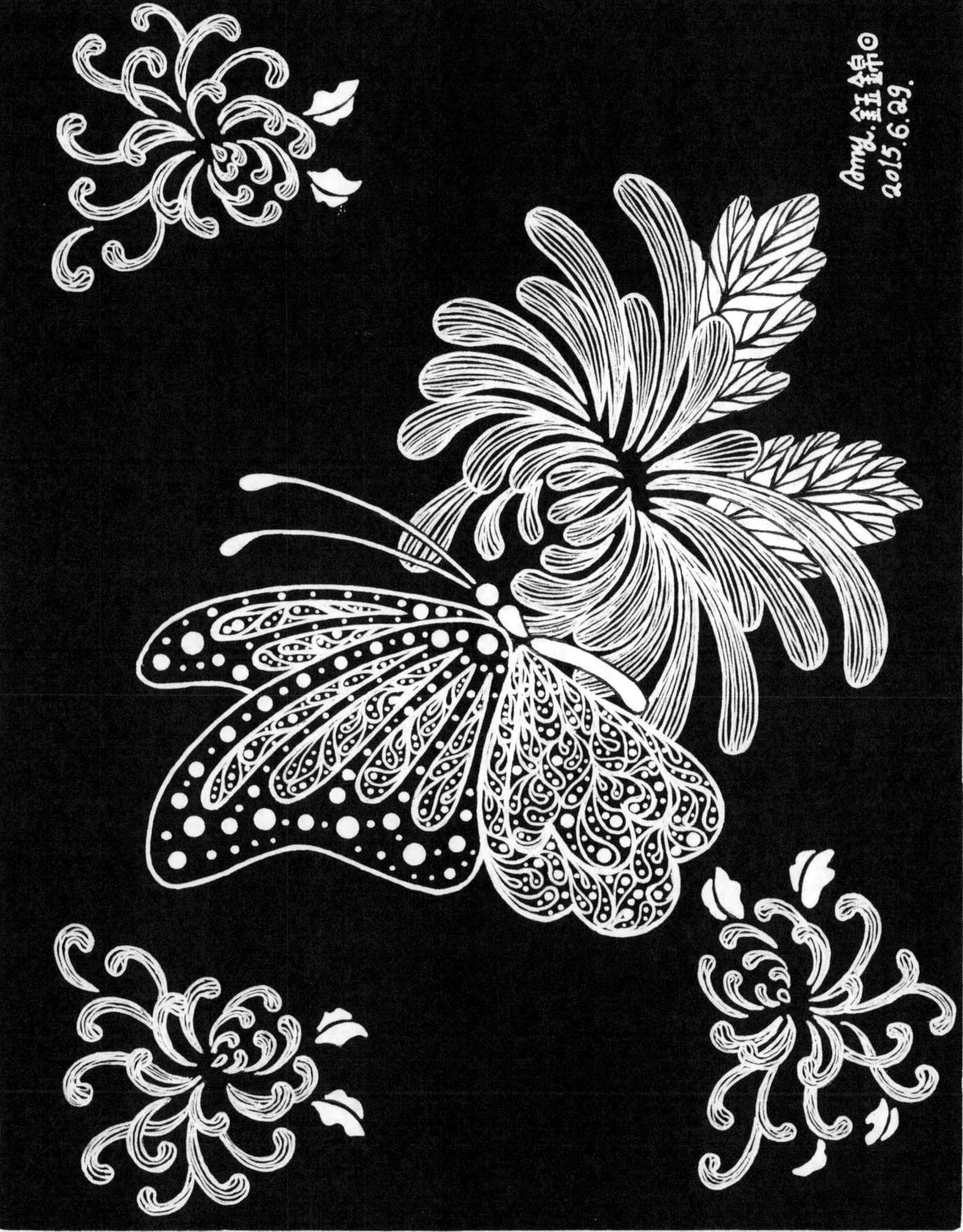

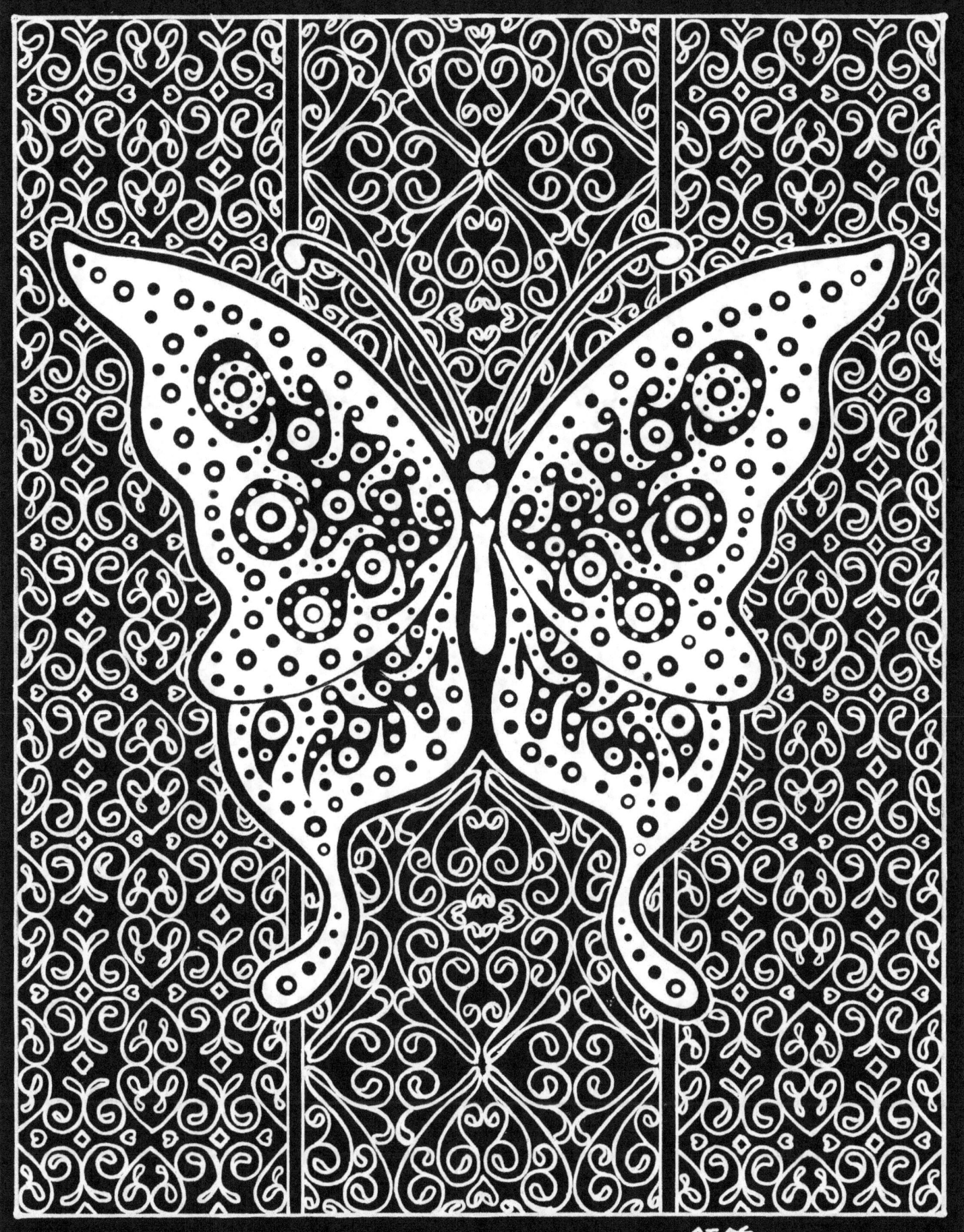

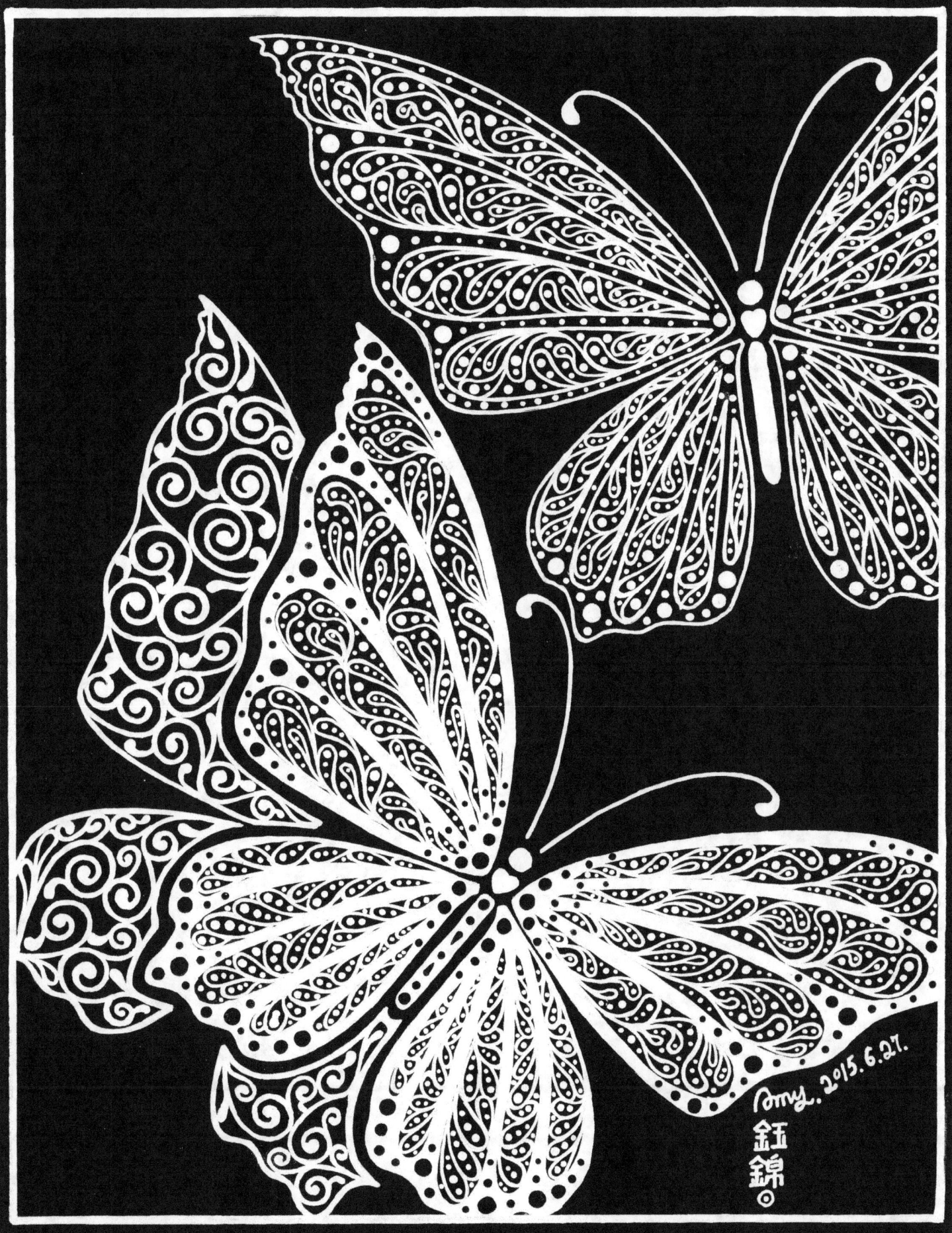

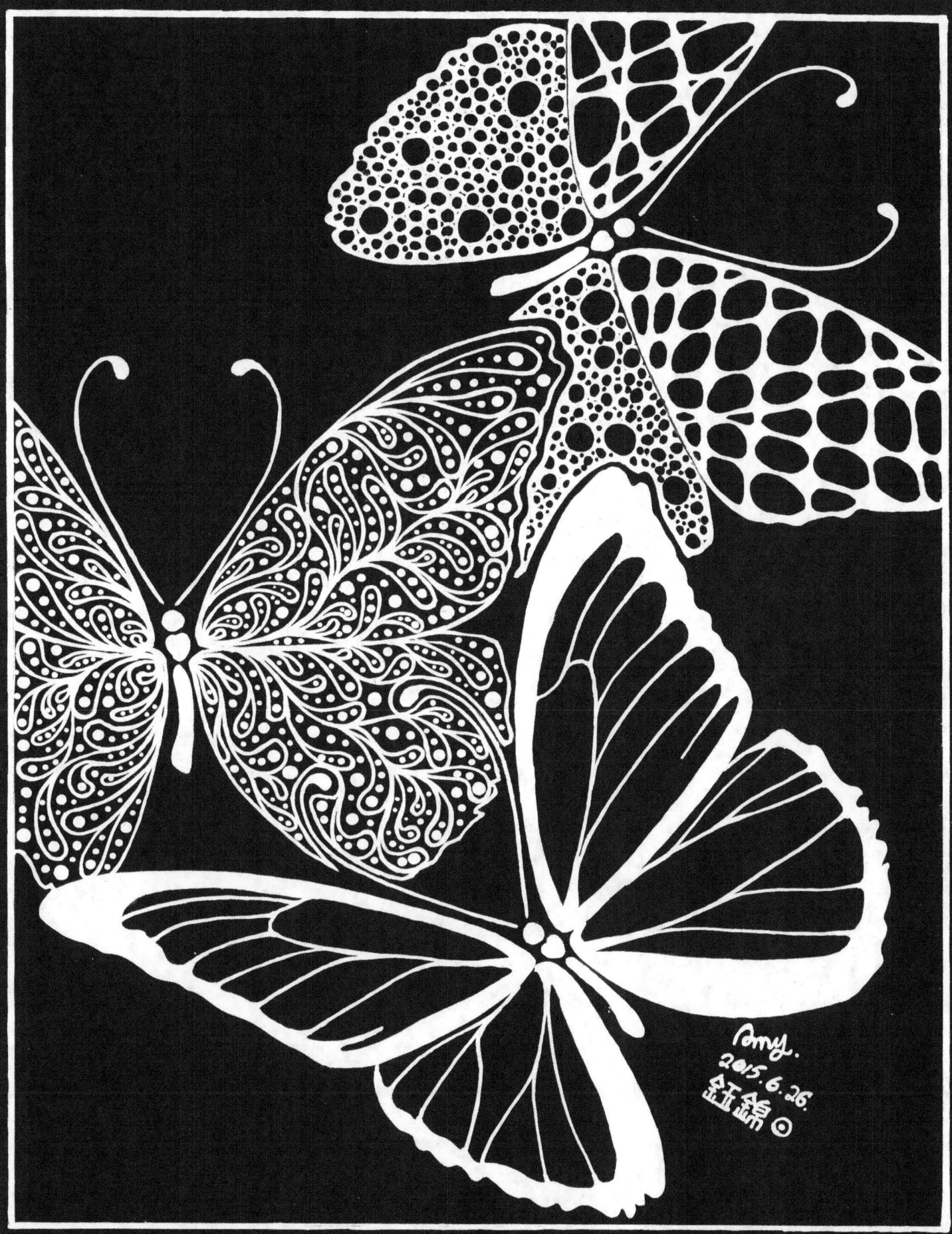

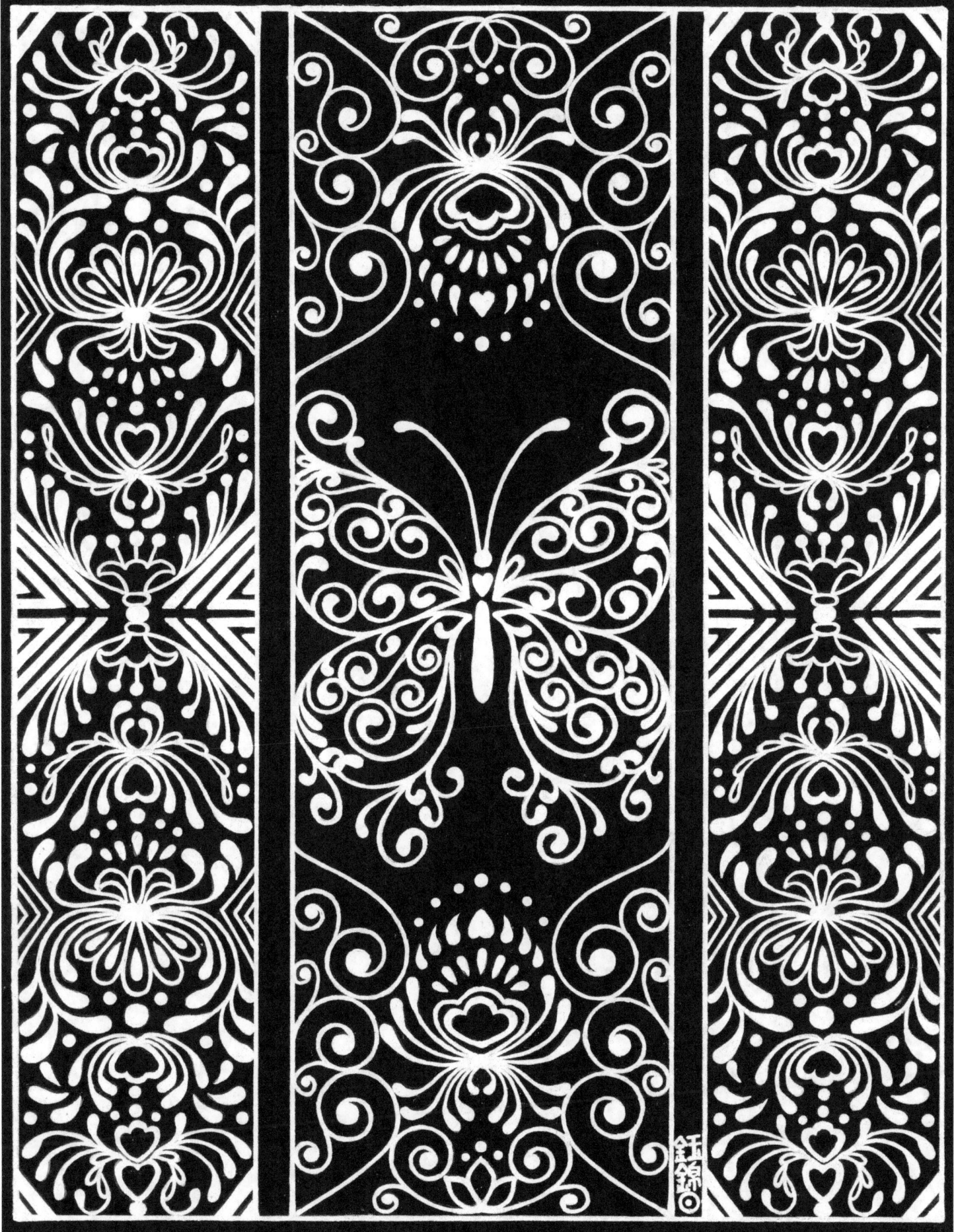

We from Global Doodle Gems, hope your journey through our book has been a pleasant one!

Please feel free to share your colored versions with us here:

https://www.facebook.com/groups/globaldoodlegems/

In our group you can meet the artists and enjoy exclusive freebies, video previews and participate in our community charity books "100 Doodles from 100 Doodlers" and so much more.... if you are wishing, that you could have the Chapter pages without the text, well then swing on by the group and get them for free in the freebie pdf for volume 11......

Are you curious about Volume 12 ?....well, just take a look at the next 2 pages and you will know what to exspect in the next volume of "Global Doodle Gems!

"Global Doodle Gems" Volume 12
Preview

Leaf Yeh

Ellen Wolters

Linda Fauconnier Tricoire

T.J.

Alexandra Rodriguez

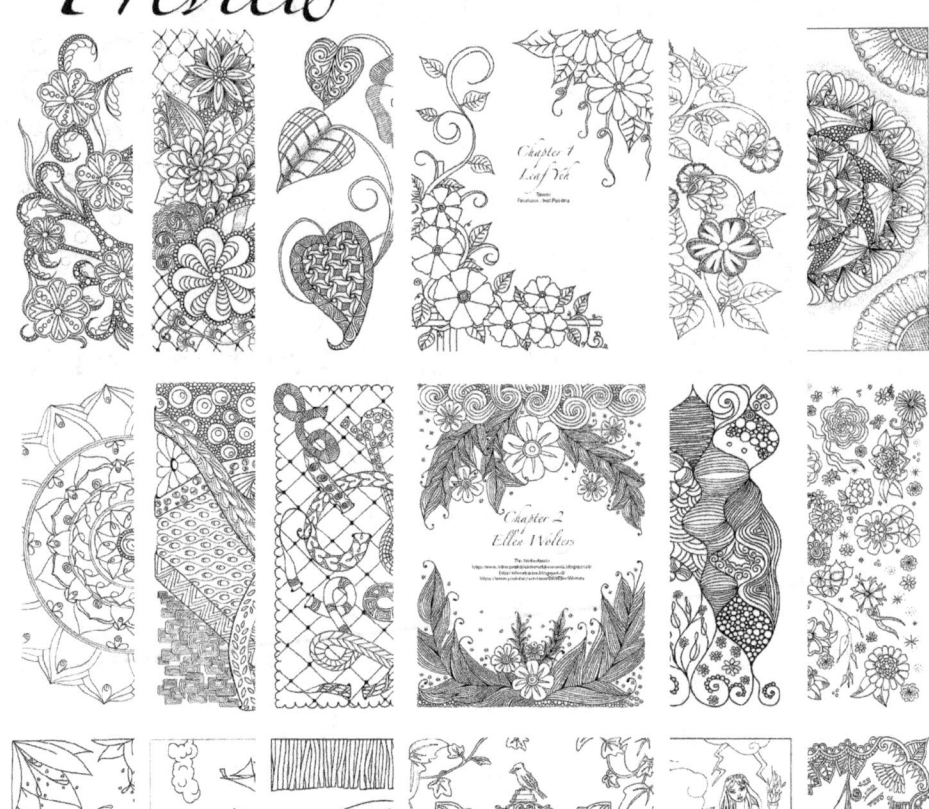
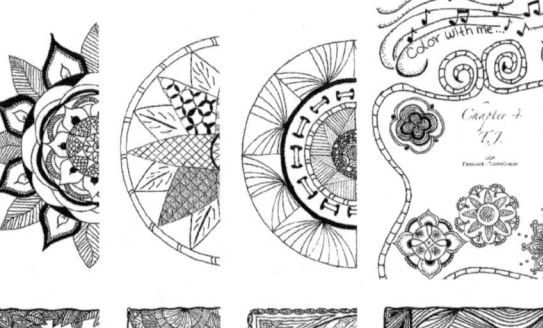
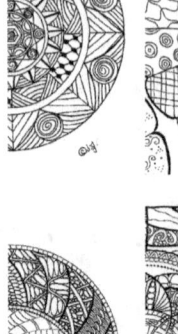
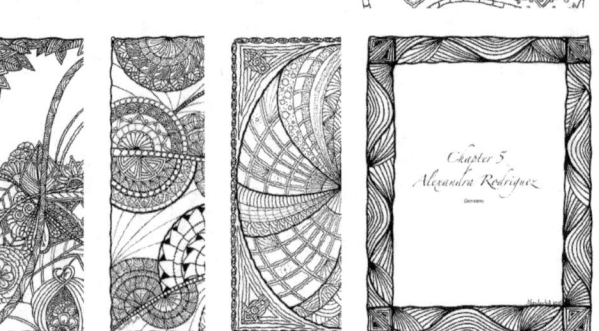
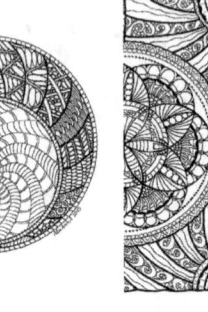

Gloria Lenzen

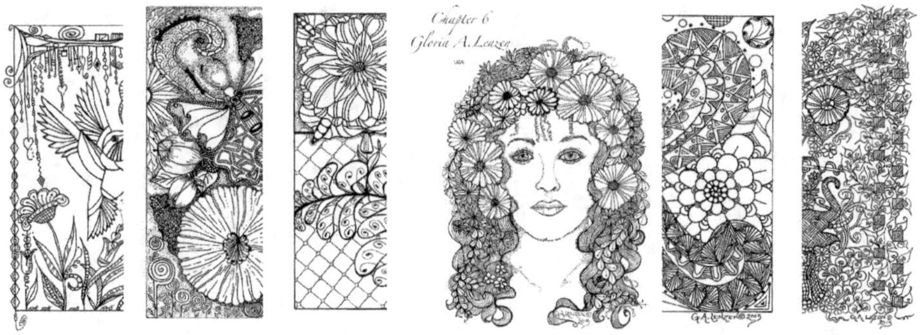

Royer Hsiao

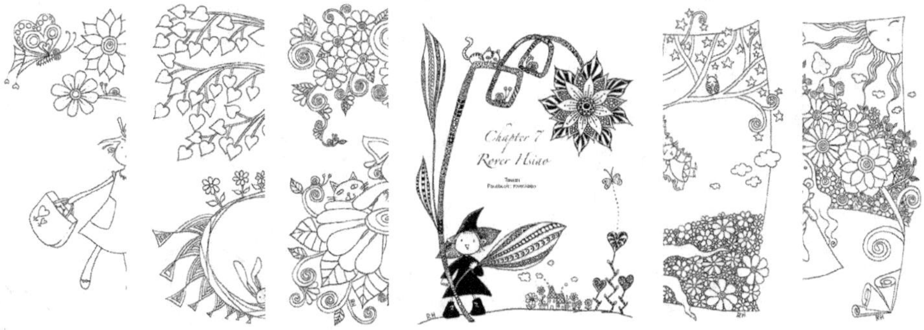

Debbie Lai

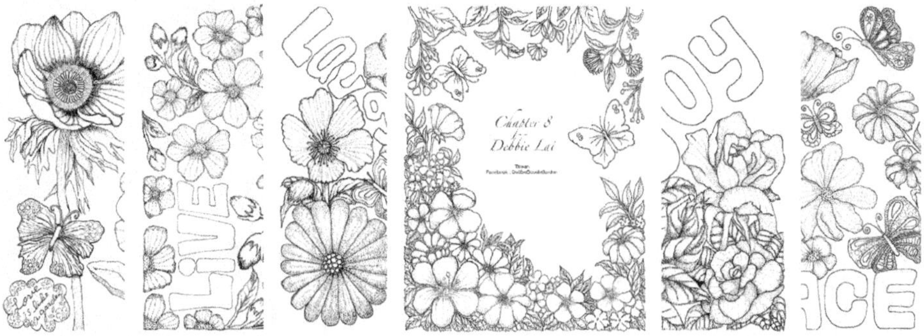

Lilan Chen

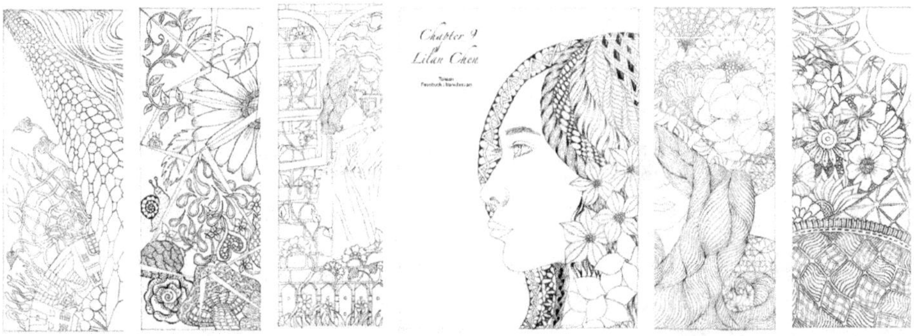

Jodi Ho

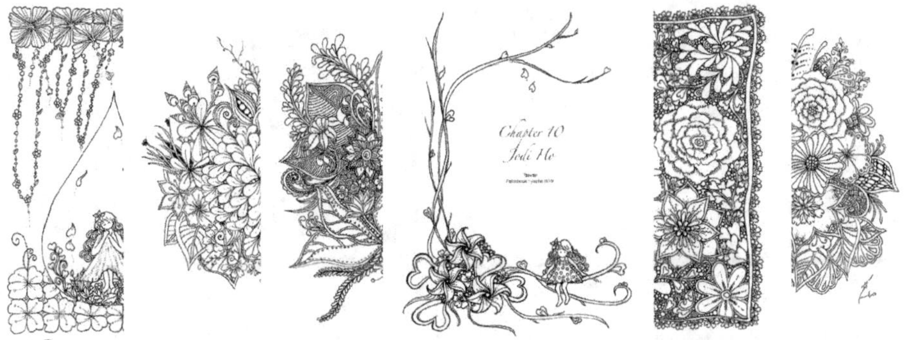

Meet the artists feautured in "GDG" Volume 12

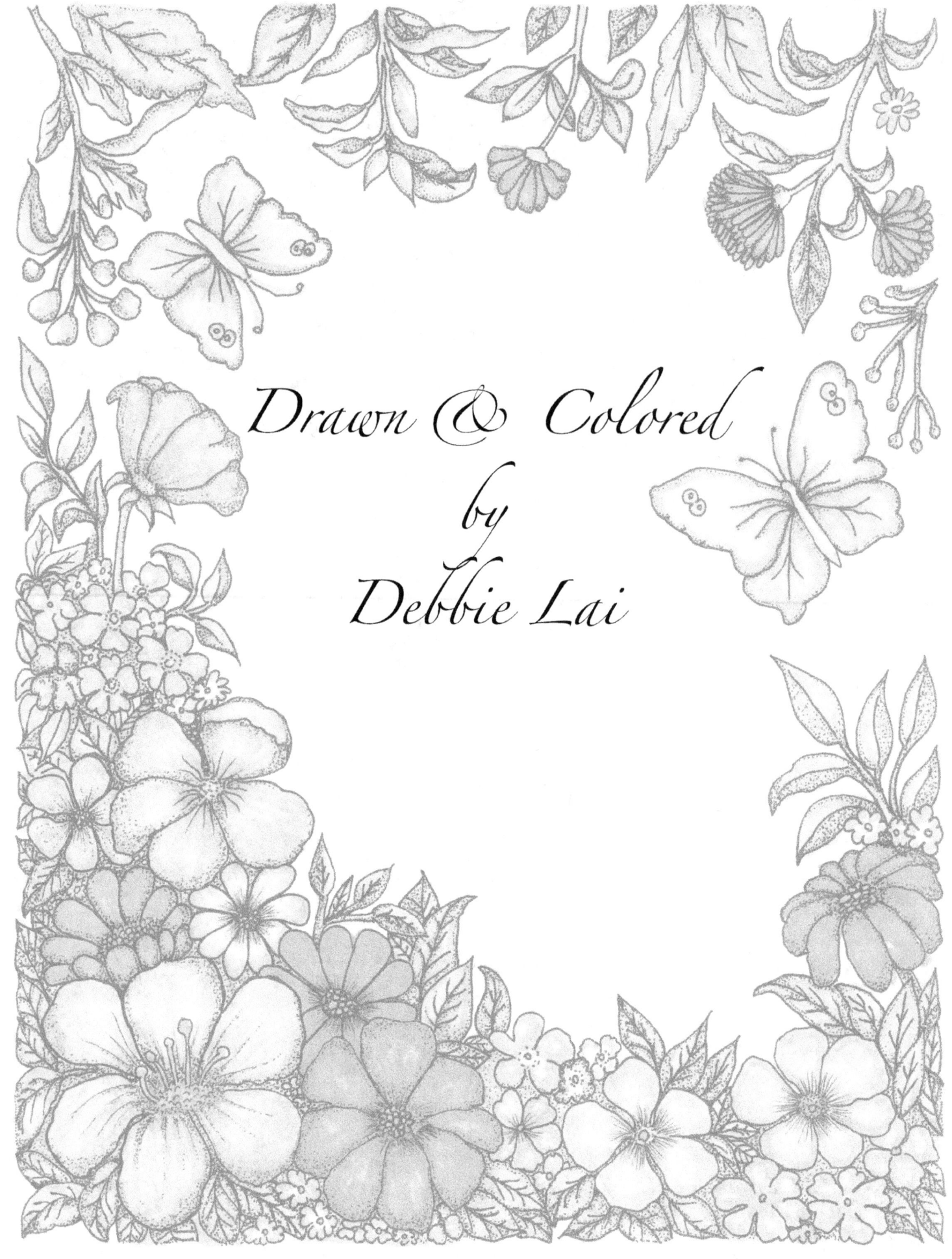

Drawn & Colored by Debbie Lai

www.ingramcontent.com/pod-product-compliance
Lightning Source LLC
Chambersburg PA
CBHW082207220526
45470CB00010B/3073